C00

D1150277

1/6/17

 libraries

Parkhead Library
64 Tollcross Road
Glasgow G31 4XA
Phone: 0141 276 1530 Fax 276 1531

This book is due for return on or before the last date shown below. It may
be renewed by telephone, personal application, fax or post, quoting this
date, author, title and the book number

15 MAR 2018

1 6 MAR 2020

WITHDRAWN

1 3 5 7 9 10 8 6 4 2

Vintage
20 Vauxhall Bridge Road,
London SW1V 2SA

Vintage Classics is part of the Penguin Random House
group of companies whose addresses can be found at
glo

Ex⟨⟩⟩8

Jul
the
De

Fir
Th

Ex⟨2006)

reproduced by kind permission of McGraw-Hill Companies, Inc.

penguin.co.uk/vintage

A CIP catalogue record for this book is available from the British Library

ISBN 9781784872601

Typeset in 9.5/14.5 pt FreightText Pro
by Jouve (UK), Milton Keynes
Printed and bound by Clays Ltd, St Ives plc

Death
JULIAN BARNES

VINTAGE MINIS

WHEN WE LET THE MIND roam to the circumstances of our own death, there is usually a magnetic pull towards the worst case or the best case. My worst imaginings usually involve enclosure, water, and a period of time in which to endure the certainty of coming extinction. There is, for instance, the overturned-ferry scenario: the air pocket, darkness, slowly rising water, screaming fellow mortals, and the competition for breath. Then there is the solitary version of this: bundled into the boot of a car (perhaps your own) while your captors drive from one cashpoint to another, and then, when your credit card is finally refused, the giddying lurch from river bank or sea cliff, the splash, and the greedy glug of water coming for you. Or the analogous, if more improbable, wildlife version of this: being taken by a crocodile, dragged under water, losing consciousness and then regaining it on a shelf above the waterline in the croc's lair, and realizing that you have just become the waiting contents of the beast's larder. (And such things happen, in case you doubt.)

The best case, in my fantasizing, used to turn on a medical diagnosis which left me just enough time, and just enough lucidity, in which to write that last book – the one which would contain all my thoughts about death. Although I didn't know if it was going to be fiction or non-fiction, I had the first line planned and noted many years ago: 'Let's get this death thing straight.' But what kind of doctor is going to give you the diagnosis that suits your literary requirements? 'I'm afraid there's good news and bad news.' 'Tell me straight, Doc, I need to know. How long?' 'How long? I'd say about 200 pages. 250 if you're lucky, or work fast.'

No, it isn't going to happen like that, so it's best to get the book done before the diagnosis. Of course, there is a third possibility: you start the book, you are nearly half-way through and then you get the diagnosis! Maybe the narrative is flagging a bit by this stage, so enter the chest pain, the fainting fit, the X-rays, the CAT scan . . . Would that, I wonder, look a little contrived? (The readers' group confers. 'Oh, I always thought he was going to die at the end – well, after the end, didn't you?' 'No, I thought he might be bluffing. I wasn't sure he was even ill. I thought it might be, what do you call it, meta-fiction?')

It probably isn't going to happen this way either. When we imagine our own dying, whether best or worst case, we tend to imagine dying lucidly, dying while aware (all too aware) of what is going on, able to express ourselves and understand others. How successfully can we imagine dying – and the long lead-up to the event itself – in a state of incoherence and misunderstanding? With the same original pain and fear, of course, but now with an added layer of confusion. Not knowing quite who anybody is, not knowing who is alive or dead, not knowing where you are. (But just as shit-scared anyway.) I remember visiting an elderly and demented friend in hospital. She would turn to me, and in her soft, rather genteel voice which I had once much loved, would say things like, 'I do think you will be remembered as one of the worst criminals in history.' Then a nurse might walk past, and her mood change swiftly. 'Of course,' she would assure me, 'the maids here are frightfully good.' Sometimes I would let such remarks pass (for her sake, for my sake), sometimes (for her sake, for my sake) correct them. 'Actually, they're nurses.' My friend would give a cunning look expressing surprise at my naivety. 'Some of them are,' she conceded. 'But *most* of them are maids.'

My father had a series of strokes which reduced him, over the years, from an erect man of my height, first to a figure hunched over a Zimmer, his head cocked in that awkward angled lift the frame compels, and then to the half-humiliated occupant of a wheelchair. When the social services came to assess his level of incapacity, they explained that he would need, and they would pay for, a handrail to help him from bed to door. My mother overrode the suggestion: 'Not having that ugly thing in the room.' She maintained that it would spoil the bungalow's decor; but her refusal was, I now suspect, an oblique way of denying what had happened – and what might await her too. One thing she did allow – to my surprise – was an alteration to Dad's armchair. This was the sturdy green high-backed Parker Knoll in which Grandpa used to read his *Daily Express*, and mistake Grandma's stomach for the telephone. Now, its legs were extended with metal sheaths, so that Dad could get in and out more easily.

This slow physical crumbling was paralleled by an erosion of my father's speech: of his articulation, and memory for words. (He had been a French teacher, and now his *langue* was going.) I see again the shuffle-and-push of his slow Zimmer progress from lounge to front door when he came to see me off: a stretch of time which felt endless, and where every conversational topic sounded utterly false. I would pretend to linger, look searchingly at a jug of flowers on the sideboard, or pause to observe again some knick-knack I had always disliked. Eventually, the three of us would make it to the front mat. On one occasion, my father's farewell words were, 'And next time, bring . . . bring . . .' Then he got stuck. I didn't know whether to wait, or, with a pretence of understanding, nod agreeingly. But my mother said firmly, 'Bring who?' – as if my father's mental fallibility were something correctible by the right sort of questioning. 'Bring . . . bring . . .' His expression was now one of furious frustration at his own brain. 'Bring *who*?' my mother repeated. By now the answer was so obvious and unnecessary that I wanted to run out of the door, jump in the car and drive away. Suddenly, Dad found a way round his aphasia. 'Bring . . . Julian's wife.' Ah, relief. But not quite. My mother, to my ear not sounding all that sympathetic, said, 'Oh, you mean P.' – thus turning my schoolmaster father into some test-failing schoolboy.

He would stand at the front door, crouched over his frame with its stupid, empty metal basket clipped to the handlebars; his head would be tilted, as if he were trying to prevent the action of gravity on his lower jaw. I would say goodbye and set off the dozen yards or so to my car, whereupon – inevitably – my mother would 'remember' something, come at a trot down the little curve of tarmac (her hurried gait emphasizing my father's immobility) and tap on the window. I would lower it reluctantly, guessing what she was going to say. 'What do you think? He's deteriorated, hasn't he?' I would look past my mother to my father, who knew we were talking about him, and knew that I knew that he knew. 'No,' I would usually reply, out of loyalty to Dad, because the only alternative would have been to bellow, 'He's had a fucking stroke, Ma, what do you expect – volleyball?' But she would judge my diplomatic reply proof of inattention, and as I slowly let out the clutch and inched my way down the tarmac, would hold on to the window and give examples of the deterioration I had failed to observe.

I do not mean that she was unkind to him; but her way

of dealing with my father's condition was to stress her own inconvenience and suffering, while implying that his suffering was a little more his own fault than people realized. 'Of course, when he falls down, he panics,' she would complain. 'Well, I can't lift him, so I have to get someone from the village to help. But he panics because he can't get up.' Black mark. Then there was the matter of my father's pedalling machine, which the hospital physiotherapist had provided. He was supposed to sit in his Parker Knoll and pump away at this shiny little bicycle remnant. Whether mock-cycling in an armchair struck my father as absurd, or whether he simply decided that it wouldn't make the slightest difference to his condition, I don't know. 'He's so stubborn,' my mother would complain.

Of course, when it came to her turn, she was just as stubborn. Her initial stroke was far more immobilizing than Dad's first one: she was largely paralysed down her right side, and her speech was more damaged than his. She showed herself most coherent when in greatest rage at what had happened. With her good hand she would reach across and pick up her stricken arm. 'And of course,' she said, sounding for a moment exactly like her old self, 'this thing's *completely useless*.' This thing had let her down, rather as my father had. And then, exactly like Dad, she treated the physiotherapists with scepticism. 'They're pushing and pulling at me,' she would complain. When I told her they were pushing and pulling at her to help her recover, she replied, satirically, 'Yes, sir.' Yet she was admirably unflinching, and dismissive of what she saw as false morale-boosting. 'They tell you to do something, and then they say, "Very good." It's so stupid, I *know* it isn't very good.' So she stopped cooperating. Her way of remaining herself was to mock professional optimism and decline the hypothetical recovery.

My niece C. went to visit her. I called to ask how it had gone, and how Ma was. 'Completely bonkers when I got there, but once we started talking about make-up, completely sane.' Suspecting the harshness of youth in my niece's assessment, I asked – perhaps a little stiffly – what form being 'bonkers' had taken. 'Oh, she was very angry with you. She said you'd stood her up three days running for tennis, and left her there on court.' OK, bonkers.

Not that my niece escaped censure. On one occasion she and I sat through twenty mysterious minutes of furious silence and stubborn avoidance of eye contact. Eventually, Ma turned to C. and said, 'You're a *proper monkey*, you are. But you do understand why I had to tear a strip off you, don't you?' Perhaps such dishing-out of fantastical blame gave her the illusion of control over her life. Blame which extended also to my brother, whose absence in France did not excuse or protect him. About two weeks after her first stroke, with her speech largely incomprehensible, we were discussing – or rather, I was telling her – how I would manage things while she was in hospital. I listed the people I could consult, adding that if there was any problem, I could always fall back on my brother's 'fine brain'. With struggling pauses between each word, our mother succeeded in putting together the flawless sentence: 'His fine brain doesn't think about anything but work.'

Despite months of stubborn non-cooperation in hospital, she recovered some of her speech, though none of her movement. Not being one to fool herself, she announced that she was incapable of returning to live in her bungalow. A staff nurse called Sally came to assess her ability to function in the nursing home C. and I were hoping to get her into. Ma claimed to have already inspected the place and found it 'pukka'; though I suspect that her 'visit' had been fabulated from reading a brochure. She told Staff Nurse Sally that she had decided to take her meals alone in her room: she couldn't eat with the other residents because she lacked the use of her right arm. 'Oh, don't be silly,' said the nurse. 'It doesn't matter.' My mother's reply was commanding: 'When I say it matters, *it matters*.' 'Have you ever been a teacher?' was Sally's canny riposte.

As a young man, I was terrified of flying. The book I would choose to read on a plane would be something I felt appropriate to have found on my corpse. I remember taking *Bouvard et Pécuchet* on a flight from Paris to London, deluding myself that after the inevitable crash a) there would be an identifiable body on which it might be found; b) that Flaubert in French paperback would survive impact and flames; c) that when recovered, it would still be grasped in my miraculously surviving (if perhaps severed) hand, a stiffened forefinger bookmarking a particularly admired passage, of which posterity would therefore take note. A likely story – and I was naturally too scared during the flight to concentrate on a novel whose ironic truths in any case tend to be withheld from younger readers.

I was largely cured of my fear at Athens airport. I was in my mid-twenties, and had arrived in good time for my flight home – such good time (so eager to leave) that instead of being several hours early, I was a whole day and several hours early. My ticket could not be changed; I had no money to go back into the city and find a hotel; so I camped out at the airport. Again, I can remember the book – the crash companion – I had with me: a volume of Durrell's Alexandria Quartet. To kill time, I went up on to the viewing roof of the terminal building. From there, I watched plane after plane take off, plane after plane land. Some of them probably belonged to dodgy airlines and were crewed by drunks; but none of them crashed. I watched scores of planes not crash. And this visual, rather than statistical, demonstration of the safety of flying convinced me.

Could I try this trick again? If I looked on death more closely and more frequently – took a job as an undertaker's assistant or mortuary clerk – might I again, by the evidence of familiarity, lose my fear? Possibly. But there's a fallacy here, which my brother, as a philosopher, would quickly point out. The fallacy is this: at Athens airport, I was watching thousands and thousands of passengers *not* die. At an undertaker's or mortuary, I would be confirming my worst suspicion: that the death rate for the human race is not a jot lower than one hundred per cent.

THERE'S ANOTHER FLAW in that 'best-case' death scenario I was describing. Let's assume the doctor says you will live long enough and lucidly enough to complete your final book. Who wouldn't drag the work out as long as possible? Scheherazade never ran out of stories. 'Morphine drip?' 'Oh no, still quite a few chapters to go. The fact is, there's a lot more to say about death than I'd imagined . . .' And so your selfish wish to survive would act to the structural detriment of the book.

Some years ago, a British journalist, John Diamond, was diagnosed with cancer, and turned his condition into a weekly column. Rightly, he maintained the same perky tone that characterized the rest of his work; rightly, he admitted cowardice and panic alongside curiosity and occasional courage. His account sounded completely authentic: this was what living with cancer entailed; nor did being ill make you a different person, or stop you having rows with your wife. Like many other readers, I used to quietly urge him on from week to week. But after a year and more . . . well, a certain narrative expectation inevitably built up. Hey, miracle cure! Hey, I was just having you on! No, neither of those would work as endings. Diamond had to die; and he duly, correctly (in narrative terms) did. Though – how can I put this? – a stern literary critic might complain that his story lacked compactness towards the end.

I may be dead by the time you are reading this sentence. In which case, any complaints about the book will not be answered. On the other hand, we may both be alive now (you by definition so), but you could die before me. Had you thought of that? Sorry to bring it up, but it is a possibility, at least for a few more years. In which case, my condolences to your nearest and dearest. And either I'll be going to your funeral, or you'll be coming to mine. Such has always been the case, of course; but this grimly unshiftable either/or takes on sharper definition in later years. In the matter of you and me – assuming I'm not already, definitively dead by the time you're reading this – you're more likely, actuarially, to see me out than the other way round. And there's still that other possibility – that I might die in the middle of writing this book. Which would be unsatisfactory for both of us – unless you were about to give up anyway, at exactly the point where the narrative breaks off. I might die in the middle of a sentence, even. Perhaps right in the middle of a wo

Just kidding. Though not entirely so. I've never written a book, except my first, without at some point considering that I might die before it was completed. This is all part of the superstition, the folklore, the mania of the business, the fetishistic fuss. The right pencils, felt-tips, biros, notebooks, paper, typewriter: necessities which are also objective correlatives for the proper state of mind. This is created by putting aside all that might harmfully impinge, narrowing the focus until only what's important remains: me, you, the world and the book – and how to make it as good as it can possibly be. Reminding myself of mortality (or, more truthfully, mortality reminding me of itself) is a useful and necessary prod.

So is advice from those who have been there before. Instructions, epigrams, dicta pinned up either literally or metaphorically. Both William Styron and Philip Roth have worked beneath the Flaubertian self-reminder: 'Be regular and ordinary in your life, like a bourgeois, so that you may be violent and original in your work.' Perhaps you need to free your mind from the distraction of future critical response? Sibelius would be a help here – 'Always remember that there is no city in Europe which contains a statue to a critic' – though my favourite comes from Ford Madox Ford: 'It is an easy job to say that an elephant, however good, is not a good warthog; for most criticism comes to that.' Many writers could benefit from that line of Jules Renard's: 'One could say of almost all works of literature that they are too long.' Further, and finally, they should expect to be misunderstood. On this, Sibelius again, with the gnomic and ironic instruction: 'Misunderstand me correctly.'

When I first began to write, I laid down for myself the rule – as part of the head-clearing, the focusing, the psychological primping and tamping – that I should write as if my parents were dead. This was not because I specifically wanted either to use or abuse them; rather, I didn't want to catch myself thinking of what might possibly offend or please them. (And in this, they were not just themselves, they were also standing for friends, colleagues, lovers, let alone warthog-describers.) The strange thing is, that though my parents are many years dead, I now need this rule more than ever.

Dying in the middle of a wo , or three-fifths of the way through a nov . My friend the nov ist Brian Moore used to fear this as well, though for an extra reason: 'Because some bastard will come along and finish it for you.' Here is a novelist's would-you-rather. Would you rather die in the middle of a book, and have some bastard finish it for you, or leave behind a work in progress that not a single bastard in the whole world was remotely interested in finishing? Moore died while at work on a novel about Rimbaud. An irony there: Rimbaud was one writer who made sure he wouldn't die in the middle of a stanza, two-thirds of the way through a *mo* , by abandoning literature half a lifetime before he died.

MY MOTHER, AN only child who became the only woman in a household whose male members had little instinct for dominance, developed a solipsism which did not decrease with age. In widowhood, she became even more of a monologuist than in the days when some polite, loving and occasionally wry response could be elicited from the Parker Knoll. Inevitably, she became more of a repetitionist too. I was sitting with her one afternoon, my mind half elsewhere, when she took me aback with a new thought. She had been reflecting, she said, on the various forms of decrepitude that might await her, and wondering if she would rather go deaf or go blind. For a moment – naively – I imagined that she was asking my opinion, but she needed no extra input: deafness, she told me, would be her choice. This was how she had argued the matter to herself: 'If I were blind, how would I do my nails?'

Death and dying generate a whole questionnaire of such would-you-rathers. For a start, would you rather know you were dying, or not know? Would you rather watch, or not watch? Aged thirty-eight, Jules Renard noted: 'Please, God, don't make me die too quickly! I shouldn't mind seeing how I die.' He wrote this on 24 January 1902, the second anniversary of the day he had travelled from Paris to Chitry to bury his brother Maurice – a brother transformed in a few silent minutes from a clerk of works complaining about the central heating system to a corpse with his head on a Paris telephone directory. A century later, the medical historian Roy Porter was asked to reflect on death: 'You know, I think it will be interesting to be conscious as one dies, because one must undergo the most extraordinary changes. Thinking, I'm dying now . . . I think I'd like to be fully conscious of it all. Because, you know, you'd just be missing out on something otherwise.' Such terminal curiosity is in a fine tradition. In 1777, the Swiss physiologist Albrecht von Haller was attended on his deathbed by a brother physician. Haller monitored his own pulse as it weakened, and died in character with the last words: 'My friend, the artery ceases to beat.' The following year, Voltaire similarly clung to his own pulse until the moment he slowly shook his head and, a few minutes later, died. An admirable death – with not a priest in sight. Not that it impressed everyone. Mozart, then in Paris, wrote to his father, 'You probably already know that that godless arch-rogue Voltaire has died like a dog, like a beast – that's his reward!' Like a dog, indeed.

Would you rather fear death or not fear it? That sounds an easy one. But how about this: what if you never gave death a thought, lived your life as if there were no tomorrow (there isn't, by the way), took your pleasure, did your work, loved your family, and then, as you were finally obliged to admit your own mortality, discovered that this new awareness of the full stop at the end of the sentence meant that the whole preceding story now made no sense at all? That if you'd fully realized to begin with that you were going to die, and what that meant, you would have lived according to quite different principles?

And then there is the other way round, perhaps my own: what if you lived to sixty or seventy with half an eye on the ever-filling pit, and then, as death approached, you found that there was, after all, *nothing to be frightened of*? What if you began to feel contentedly part of the great cycle of nature (please, take my carbon atoms)? What if those easeful metaphors suddenly, or even gradually, began to convince? The Anglo-Saxon poet compared human life to a bird flying from darkness into a brightly lit banqueting hall, and then flying out into the dark on the farther side: perhaps this image will calm one's pang at being human and being mortal. I can't say it works for me yet. It's pretty enough, but the pedantic side of me keeps wanting to point out that any right-thinking bird flying into a warm banqueting hall would perch on the rafters as long as it bloody well could, rather than head straight out again. Moreover, the bird, in its pre- and post-existence on either side of the carousing hall, is at least still *flying*, which is more than can or will be said for us.

When I first came to mortal awareness, it was simple: you were alive, then you were dead, and bid the Deity fare-well: Godbye. But who can tell how age will affect us? When I was a young journalist, I interviewed the novelist William Gerhardie. He was then in his eighties, frail and bed-bound; death was not far away. At one point he picked up from his bedside table an anthology about immortality, and showed me a heavily underlined account of an out-of-body experience. This, he explained, was identical to one he had himself undergone as a soldier in the First World War. 'I believe in resurrection,' he said simply. 'I believe in immortality. Do you believe in immortality?' I was awkwardly silent (and failed to remember my own out-of-body experience as a schoolboy). 'No, well, nor did I at your age,' he went on sympathetically. 'But I do now.'

So perhaps I shall change my mind (though I doubt it). What's more likely is that the choice ahead will blur. Life versus Death becomes, as Montaigne pointed out, Old Age versus Death. What you – I – will be clinging on to is not a few more minutes in a warm baronial hall with the smell of roast chicken and the cheery noise of fife and drum, not a few more days and hours of real living, but a few more days and hours of breathing decrepitude, mind gone, muscles wasted, bladder leaking. And yet – and worse – imagine this failing body now even more fearful of oblivion than when it was healthy and strong and could divert itself from contemplation of that oblivion by physical and mental activity, by social usefulness and the company of friends. A body, the compartments of whose mind now begin shutting down one by one, lucidity gone, speech gone, recognition of friends gone, memory gone, replaced by a fantasy world of proper monkeys and unreliable tennis partners. All that is left – the last bit of the engine still with stoking power – is the compartment that makes us fear death. Yes, that little bit of brain activity will keep going strong, puffing out the panic, sending the chill and the terror coursing through the system. They will give you morphine for your pain – and then, perhaps, a little more than you actually need, and then the necessary excess – but there is nothing they can give you to stop this grim cluster of brain cells scaring you shitless (or, perhaps, the opposite) until the very end. Then we might find ourselves regretting that we ever thought, with Renard, 'Please, God, don't make me die too quickly.'

The writer and director Jonathan Miller trained as a doctor. Despite having dissected the rigid and handled the waxily pliable from whom the breath of life had only just departed, he was in his forties before, as he put it, 'I began to think, well, hang on – this is something which I'm going to be doing some time.' Interviewed in his mid-fifties, he professed himself still unalarmed by the long-term conse- quences: 'The fear of just not existing – no, I don't have that at all.' What he admitted to instead was a fear of the deathbed, and what goes with it: agony, delirium, torturing hallucinations, and the lamenting family preparing for his departure. That seems a pretty fair line-up to me, though not as an alternative, merely as an add-on to the proper, grown-up fear of 'just not existing'.

Miller follows Freud in that he 'cannot actually con- ceive, can't make sense of the notion of total annihilation'. And so, it seems, his capacity for terror is transferred first on to the process and humiliations of dying, and secondly on to various possible states of semi-being or almost-being which might occur around or after death. He fears 'this residual consciousness which is not quite snuffed out', and imagines an out-of-body experience in which he is watch- ing his own funeral: 'or, in fact, not watching it, but being immobilized inside the coffin'. I can picture this new tweak on that old fear of being buried alive, but fail to find it especially sinister. If there were a residual consciousness watching our own funeral and rippling around inside our coffin, why should it necessarily be one that fears enclosure?

Most of us have thought, or said, of death, 'Well, we shall find out' – while recognizing the near certainty that we shall never 'find out' the negative we expect. A lingering consciousness might be there to give us the answer. It might be a gentle way of saying No. It might hoveringly watch the burial or cremation, farewell this pesky body of ours and the life that has been in it, and (assuming that it is still somehow attached to or representative of the self) allow 'us' to feel that what is happening is appropriate. It might produce a calming sensation, a laying-to-rest, a consolation, a sweet goodnight, an ontological nightcap.

I have a Swedish friend, K., who once, very gently and considerately, whispered to a mutual friend who had been too long dying of cancer, 'It's time to let go.' I have always teased her that I shall know things are really bad for me when I hear this lightly inflected voice in my ear, and those much-rehearsed words of advice. Perhaps the residual consciousness that Miller fears will turn out to be something useful and benevolent, a settling of accounts delivered in a soft Swedish accent.

THAT MEDIEVAL BIRD flies from darkness into a lighted hall and back out again. One of the oh-so-sensible arguments against death-anxiety goes like this: if we don't fear and hate the eternity of time leading up to our brief moment of illuminated life, why therefore should we feel differently about the second spell of darkness? *Because*, of course, during that first spell of darkness, the universe – or at least, a very, very insignificant part of it – was leading up to the creation of something of decided interest, plaiting its genes appropriately and working its way through a succession of apelike, growling, tool-handling ancestors until such time as it gathered itself and spat out the three generations of schoolteachers who then made . . . me. So that darkness had some purpose – at least, from my solipsistic point of view; whereas the second darkness has absolutely nothing to be said for it.

It could, I suppose, be worse. It almost always can – which is some mild consolation. We might fear the prenatal abyss as well as the post-mortal one. Odd, but not impossible. Nabokov in his autobiography describes a 'chronophobiac' who experienced panic on being shown home movies of the world in the months before he was born: the house he would inhabit, his mother-to-be leaning out of a window, an empty pram awaiting its occupant. Most of us would be unalarmed, indeed cheered, by all this; the chronophobiac saw only a world in which he did not exist, an acreage of himlessness. Nor was it any consolation that such an absence was mobilizing itself irresistibly to produce his future presence. Whether this phobia reduced his level of post-mortal anxiety, or on the other hand doubled it, Nabokov does not relate.

A more sophisticated version of the bird-in-hall argument comes from Richard Dawkins. We are indeed all going to die, and death is absolute and God a delusion, but even so, that makes us the lucky ones. Most 'people' – the vast majority of potential people – don't even get born, and their numbers are greater than all the grains of sand in all the deserts of Araby. 'The set of possible people allowed by our DNA . . . massively exceeds the set of actual people. In the teeth of these stupefying odds it is you and I, in our ordinariness, that are here.' Why do I find this such thin consolation? No, worse than that, such a disconsolation? Because look at all the evolutionary work, all the unrecorded pieces of cosmic luck, all the decision-making, all the generations of family care, all the thissing-and-thatting which have ended up producing me and my uniqueness. My ordinariness, too, and yours, and that of Richard Dawkins, yet a unique ordinariness, a staggeringly against-the-odds ordinariness. This makes it harder, not easier, to give a shrug and say philosophically, Oh well, might never have been here anyway, so may as well get on enjoying this little window of opportunity not granted to others. But then it's also hard, unless you're a biologist, to think of those trillions of unborn, genetically hypothetical others as 'potential people'. I have no difficulty imagining a still-born or aborted baby as a potential person, but all those possible combinations that never came to pass? My human sympathy can only go so far, I'm afraid – the sands of Araby are beyond me.

So I cannot be philosophical. Are philosophers philo-sophical? Were the Laconians truly laconic, the Spartans really spartan? Just in comparative terms, I expect. Apart from my brother, the only philosopher I know well is my death-haunted friend G., who as a four-year-old beat me to mortal awareness by a decade. He and I once had a long exchange about free will. Like everyone, I have always – an amateur in and of my own life – assumed that I had free will, and always, to my own mind, behaved as if I did. Pro-fessionally, G. explained to me my delusion. He pointed out that though we might think we are free in acting as we want, we cannot determine what it is that we want (and if we deliberately decide to 'want to want' something, there is the usual problem of regression to a primal 'want'). At some point your wants must just be givens: the result of inheritance and upbringing. Therefore, the idea of anyone having true and ultimate responsibility for their acts is untenable; at most we can have a temporary, surface responsibility – and even that, with time, will be shown to be mistaken. G. might well have quoted to me Einstein's conclusion that 'a Being endowed with higher insight and more perfect intelligence, watching man and his doings, would smile about man's illusion that he was acting according to his own free will'.

At a certain point, I admitted that I had lost the argu-ment, though carried on behaving in exactly the same way (which, on reflection, might have been a useful proof of G.'s point). G. consoled me by remarking that though, in his philosophical opinion, we cannot possibly have free will, such knowledge doesn't make the slightest practical difference to how we do, or even should, behave. And so I have continued to rely on this delusionary mental construct to help me along the mortal path to that place where no will of mine, free or fettered, will ever operate again.

There is What We Know (or think we know) To Be The Case, there is What We Believe To Be The Case (on the assurance of others whom we trust), and then there is How We Behave. Christian morality still loosely governs Britain, though congregations dwindle and church buildings make their inexorable transition to historic monuments – setting off in some 'a hunger to be serious' – and loft apartments. That sway extends to me too: my sense of morality is influenced by Christian teaching (or, more exactly, pre-Christian tribal behaviour codified by the religion); and the God I don't believe in yet miss is naturally the Christian God of Western Europe and non-fundamentalist America. I don't miss Allah or Buddha, any more than I miss Odin or Zeus. And I miss the New Testament God rather than the Old Testament one. I miss the God that inspired Italian painting and French stained glass, German music and English chapter houses, and those tumbledown heaps of stone on Celtic headlands which were once symbolic beacons in the darkness and the storm. I also realize that this God I am missing, this inspirer of artworks, will seem to some just as much an irrelevant self-indulgence as the much-claimed 'own personal idea of God'. Further, if any God did exist, He might very well find such decorative celebration of His existence both trivial and vainglorious, a matter for divine indifference if not retribution. He might think Fra Angelico cutesy, and Gothic cathedrals blustering attempts to impress Him by a creation which had quite failed to guess how He preferred to be worshipped.

MY AGNOSTIC AND atheistic friends are indistinguishable from my professedly religious ones in honesty, generosity, integrity and fidelity – or their opposites. Is this a victory for them, I wonder, or for us? When we are young, we think we are inventing the world as we are inventing ourselves; later, we discover how much the past holds us, and always did. I escaped what seemed to me the decent dullness of my family, only to find, as I grow older, that my resemblance to my dead father strikes me more and more. There is the angle I sit at a table, the hang of my jaw, the incipient baldness pattern, and a particular kind of polite laugh I emit when not really amused: these (and doubtless much else that I fail to pick up) are genetic replicas and definitely not expressions of free will. My brother finds the same: he talks more and more like our father, using the same slang and half-finished sentences – he catches himself 'sounding just like him, and even shuffling in my slippers the way he used to'. He has also started to dream about Dad – after sixty years in which neither parent intruded upon his sleep.

Grandma, in her dementia, believed my mother was a

sister of hers who had been dead for fifty years. My mother, in turn, welcomed back all the relatives she had known in childhood, come to express concern for her. In time, our family will come for my brother and for me (only please don't send my mother). But did the past ever really relax its grasp? We live broadly according to the tenets of a religion we no longer believe in. We live as if we are creatures of pure free will when philosophers and evolutionary biologists tell us this is largely a fiction. We live as if the memory were a well-built and efficiently staffed left-luggage office. We live as if the soul – or spirit, or individuality, or personality – were an identifiable and locatable entity rather than a story the brain tells itself. We live as if nature and nurture were equal parents when the evidence suggests that nature has both the whip hand and the whip.

Will such knowledge sink in? How long will it take? Some scientists think we shall never entirely decipher the mysteries of consciousness because all we can use to understand the brain is the brain itself. Perhaps we shall never abandon the illusion of free will because it would take an act of the free will we don't have to abandon our belief in it. We shall go on living as if we are the full arbiters of our every decision. (The various adjustments of grammar and sense that I made to that last sentence, both immediately in the writing and after subsequent time and thought – how can 'I' not believe that 'I' made them? How can I believe that those words, and this parenthesis which follows them, and every elaboration I make within

it, and the occasional misytpings, and the next word,
whether completed or abandoned-halfway-through-as-I-
have-second-thoughts-about-it and left as a wo , are not
emanations of a coherent self making literary decisions by
a process of free will? I cannot get my head round this not
being the case.)

Perhaps it will be easier for you, or if not you, the generations born after you are dead. Perhaps I – and you – will
seem to them like the 'old-type *natural* fouled-up guys'
(and gals) of Larkin's poem. Perhaps they will regard as
quaint and complacent the half-assumed, half-worked-out
morality by which you and I seem to think we live. When
religion first began to collapse in Europe – when 'godless
arch-rogues' like Voltaire were at work – there was a natural apprehension about where morality was to come
from. In a dangerously ungoverned world, every village
might produce its Casanova, its Marquis de Sade, its
Bluebeard. There were philosophers who, while refuting
Christianity to their own satisfaction and that of their
intellectual circle, believed that the knowledge should be
kept from peasant and potboy, lest the social structure collapse and the servant problem get completely out of hand.

But Europe stumbled on nonetheless. And if the
dilemma now seems to pose itself in an even sharper
form – what is the meaning of my actions in an empty universe where even more certainties have been undermined?
why behave well? why not be selfish and greedy and blame
it all on DNA? – the anthropologists and evolutionary

biologists are able to offer comfort (if not to the faithful). Whatever religions may claim, we are set up – genetically programmed – to operate as social beings. Altruism is evolutionary useful (ah! – there's your virtue – another illusion – gone); so whether or not there is a preacher with a promise of heaven and a threat of hellfire, individuals living in societies generally act in much the same way. Religion no more makes people behave better than it makes them behave worse – which might be a disappointment to the aristocratic atheist as much as to the believer.

WHEN I WAS first studying French literature, I was puzzled by the concept of the *acte gratuit*. As I understood it, the notion went like this: in order to assert that we are now in charge of the universe, we must perform a spontaneous action for which there is no apparent motive or justification, and which lies outside conventional morality. The example that I recall, from Gide's *Les Caves du Vatican*, consisted of the gratuitous actor pushing a complete stranger out of a moving train. Pure act, you see (and also, I now realize, a supposed proof of free will). I didn't see – or not enough. I found myself thinking about the unfortunate fellow dashed to death in the middle of the French countryside. Murder – or, perhaps, what bourgeois minds still mired in Christianity chose to call murder – as a means of demonstrating a philosophical point seemed too . . . too theoretical, too French, too repellent. Though my friend G. would say that the gratuitous actor would have been fooling himself (merely 'wanting to want' something). And I suppose that if his assertion of pure free will was a delusion, then so too was my reaction.

Emperor penguins have been in fashion lately, with cinematic and TV voiceovers urging us to anthropomorphism. How can we resist their loveably incompetent bipedalism? See how they rest lovingly on one another's breasts, shuffle a precious egg between parental feet, share the food search just as we share supermarket duties. Watch how the whole group huddles together against the snowstorm, demonstrating social altruism. Are we like those Antarctic penguins, or are they like us? We go to the supermarket, they slither and wobble across miles of ice to the open sea in search of food. But here is one detail the wildlife programmes omit. When the penguins approach the water's edge, they begin to dawdle and loiter. They have reached food, but also danger; the sea contains fish, but also seals. Their long journey might result not in eating but getting eaten – in which case their offspring back in the penguin-huddle will starve to death and their own gene pool be terminated. So this is what the penguins do: they wait until one of their number, either more hungry or more anxious, gets to where the ice runs out, and is gazing down into the nutritious yet deadly ocean, and then, like a gang of commuters on a station platform, they nudge the imprudent bird into the sea. Hey, just testing! This is what those loveable, anthropomorphizable penguins are 'really like'. And if we are shocked, they are at least behaving more rationally – more usefully, even more altruistically – than the gratuitous actor of our own species pushing a man from a train.

That penguin doesn't have a would-you-rather. It is plunge or die – sometimes plunge and die. And some of our own would-you-rathers turn out to be equally hypothetical: ways of simplifying the unthinkable, pretending to control the uncontrollable. My mother considered quite seriously whether she would rather go deaf or go blind. Preferring one incapacity in advance seemed a superstitious method of ruling out the other. Except that, as it turned out, the 'choice' never arose. Her stroke affected neither her hearing nor her sight – and yet she never did her nails again in what was left of her life.

My brother hopes for Grandpa's death: felled by a stroke while gardening. He fears the other family examples: Grandma's long drawn out senility, Dad's slow confinement and humiliation, Ma's half-self-aware delusions. But there are so many other possibilities to choose from – or to have chosen for us; so many different doors, even if they are all marked Exit. In this respect, death is multiple-choice not would-you-rather, and prodigally democratic in its options.

Stravinsky said: 'Gogol died screaming and Diaghilev died laughing, but Ravel died gradually. That is the worst.' He was right. There have been more violent artistic deaths, ones involving madness, terror, and banal absurdity (Webern shot dead by a GI after politely stepping on to

There are so many other possibilities to choose from – or to have chosen for us; so many different doors, even if they are all marked Exit the porch to light a cigar), but few as cruel as that of Ravel. Worse, it had a strange prefiguration – a musical pre-echo – in the death of a French composer of the previous generation. Emmanuel Chabrier had succumbed to tertiary syphilis in 1894, the year after the Paris premiere of his only attempt at serious opera, *Gwendoline*. This piece – perhaps the only opera to be set in eighth-century Britain – had taken ten years to be staged; by which time Chabrier's disease was in its final phase, and his mind in never-never land. He sat in his box at the premiere, acknowledging the applause and smiling 'almost without knowing why'. Sometimes, he would forget the opera was his, and murmur to a neighbour, 'It's good, it's really very good.'

This story was well-known among the next generation of French composers. 'Horrible, isn't it?' Ravel used to say. 'To go to a performance of *Gwendoline* and not recognize your own music!' I remember my friend Dodie Smith, in great age, being asked the tender, encouraging question, 'Now, Dodie, you do remember that you used to be a famous playwright?' To which she replied, 'Yes, I *think* so' – in rather the tone I imagine my father using when he said to my mother, 'I think you're my wife.' A milliner might not recognize her own hat, a labourer his own speed bump, a writer her words, a painter his canvas; this is poignant enough. But there is extra pain, for those who witness it, when a composer fails to recognize his own notes.

Ravel died gradually – it took five years – and it was the worst. At first his decline from Pick's disease (a form of cerebral atrophy), though alarming, was non-specific. Words evaded him; motor skills went awry. He would grasp a fork by the wrong end; he became unable to sign his name; he forgot how to swim. When he went out to dinner, the housekeeper used to pin his address inside his coat as a precaution. But then the disease turned malignly particular and targeted Ravel the composer. He went to a recording of his string quartet, sat in the control room, offered various corrections and suggestions. After each movement had been recorded, he was asked if he wanted to listen through again, but declined. So the session went quickly, and the studio was pleased to have it all wrapped up in an afternoon. At the end, Ravel turned to the producer (and our guessing what he is going to say cannot lessen its impact): 'That was really very good. Remind me of the composer's name.' Another day, he went to a concert of his piano music. He sat through it with evident pleasure, but when the hall turned to acclaim him, he thought they were addressing the Italian colleague at his side, and so joined in their applause.

Ravel was taken to two leading French neurosurgeons. Another would-you-rather. The first judged his condition inoperable, and said that nature should be allowed to take its course. The second would have agreed had the patient been anyone but Ravel. However, if there were the slightest chance – for him a few more years, for us a little more music (which is 'the best way of digesting time' according to Stravinsky) . . . And so the composer's skull was opened up, and the damage seen to be extensive and irreparable. Ten days later, his head still turbanned with hospital windings, Ravel died.

ABOUT TWENTY YEARS ago I was asked if I would be interviewed for a book about death. I declined on writerly grounds: I didn't want to talk away stuff which I might later need myself. I never read the book when it came out: perhaps from a superstitious – or rational – fear that one of its contributors might have better expressed what I was slowly working my way towards. Not long ago, I began cautiously browsing the first chapter, an interview with a certain 'Thomas'. Except that it became instantly clear, after scarcely a page, that this 'Thomas' was none other than my old death-friend and free-will eradicator G.

The primal would-you-rather about death (though again one in which we don't have the choice) is: ignorance or knowledge? Would you prefer to receive *le réveil mortel* or to slumber on in quilted blindness? This might seem an easy one: if in doubt, opt for knowledge. But it's the knowledge that causes the damage. As 'Thomas'/G. puts it: 'People who aren't afraid, I think most of them just don't know what death *means* . . . The standard theory of moral philosophy is that it's a great evil for a person to be suddenly cut off [in the flower of life]; but it seems to me that the evil is knowing it's going to happen. If it happened without your knowing, it wouldn't matter.' Or at least, it would make us more akin to those penguins: the dupe who toddles to the water's edge and is shouldered in by a non-gratuitous nudge may fear the seal but cannot conceptualize the eternal consequences of the seal.

G. has no difficulty understanding, or believing, that human beings, in all their complexity, simply disappear for ever. It is all part of 'the profligacy of nature', like the micro-engineering of a mosquito. 'I think of it as nature sort of wildly over-shooting, splurging her gifts around; with human beings it's just more of the same kind of profligacy. These extraordinary brains and sensibilities, produced in millions, and then just thrown away, disappearing into eternity. I don't think man's a special case, I think the theory of evolution explains it all. It's a very beautiful theory, come to think of it, a marvellous and inspiring theory, though it has grim consequences for us.'

That's my man! And perhaps a sense of death is like a sense of humour. We all think the one we've got – or haven't got – is just about right, and appropriate to the proper understanding of life. It's everyone else who's out of step. I think my sense of death – which appears exaggerated to some of my friends – is quite proportionate. For me, death is the one appalling fact which defines life; unless you are constantly aware of it, you cannot begin to understand what life is about; unless you know and feel that the days of wine and roses are limited, that the wine will madeirize and the roses turn brown in their stinking water before all are thrown out for ever – including the jug – there is no context to such pleasures and interests as come your way on the road to the grave. But then I would say that, wouldn't I? My friend G. has a worse case of death, so I find his hauntedness excessive, not to say unhealthy (ah, the 'healthy' attitude to it all – where is that to be found?).

For G. our only defence against death – or rather, against the danger of not being able to think about anything else – lies in 'the acquisition of worthwhile short-term worries'. He also consolingly quotes a study showing that fear of death drops off after the age of sixty. Well, I have got there before him, and can report that I am still waiting for the benefit. Only a couple of nights ago, there came again that alarmed and alarming moment, of being pitchforked back into consciousness, awake, alone, utterly alone, beating pillow with fist and shouting 'Oh no Oh No OH NO' in an endless wail, the horror of the moment – the minutes – overwhelming what might, to an objective witness, appear a shocking display of exhibitionist self-pity. An inarticulate one, too: for what sometimes shames me is the extraordinary lack of descriptive, or responsive, words that come out of my mouth. For God's sake, you're a *writer*, I say to myself. You do *words*. Can't you improve on that? Can't you face down death – well, you won't ever face it down, but can't you at least protest against it – more interestingly than this? We know that extreme physical pain

For me, death is the one appalling fact which defines life

drives out language; it's dispiriting to learn that mental pain does the same.

I once read that Zola was similarly startled from his bed like a projectile, launched from sleep into mortal terror. In my unpublished twenties, I used to think of him fraternally – and also with apprehension: if this stuff is still happening to a world-famous writer in his fifties, then there's not much chance of it getting better for me with the years. The novelist Elizabeth Jane Howard once told me that the three most death-haunted people she had ever known were her ex-husband Kingsley Amis, Philip Larkin and John Betjeman. Tempting to conclude that it might be a writer thing, even a male writer thing. Amis used to maintain – comically, given his biography – that men were more sensitive than women.

I very much doubt it – both the male thing, and the writer thing. I used to believe, when I was 'just' a reader, that writers, because they wrote books where truth was found, because they described the world, because they saw into the human heart, because they grasped both the particular and the general and were able to re-create both in free yet structured forms, because they *understood*, must therefore be more sensitive – also less vain, less selfish – than other people. Then I became a writer, and started meeting other writers, and studied them, and concluded that the only difference between them and other people, the only, single way in which they were better, was that they were better writers. They might indeed be sensitive, perceptive, wise, generalizing and particularizing – but only at their desks and in their books. When they venture out into the world, they regularly behave as if they have left all their comprehension of human behaviour stuck in their typescripts. It's not just writers either. How wise are philosophers in their private lives?

'Not a whit wiser for being philosophers,' replies my brother. 'Worse, in their semi-public lives, far less wise than many other species of academics.' I remember once laying down Bertrand Russell's autobiography in a moment, not of disbelief, more a kind of appalled belief. This is how he describes the beginning of the end of his first marriage: 'I went out bicycling one afternoon, and suddenly, as I was riding along a country road, I realized that I no longer loved Alys. I had no idea until this moment that my love for her was even lessening.' The only logical response to this, to its implications and manner of expression, would be: keep philosophers off bicycles. Or perhaps, keep philosophers out of marriage. Save them for discussing truth with God. I would want Russell on my side for that.

ON MY SIXTIETH birthday, I have lunch with T., one of my few religious friends. Or do I just mean faith-professing? Anyway, he is Catholic, wears a cross around his neck and, to the alarm of some past girlfriends, has a crucifix on the wall above his bed. Yes, that does sound more like religious than faith-professing, I know. T. is soon to marry R., who may or may not have the power to remove the crucifix. This being my birthday, I allow myself more interrogatory latitude, so ask why – apart from having been brought up as a Catholic – he believes in his God and his religion. He thinks for a while and replies, 'I believe because I want to believe.' Sounding perhaps a little like my brother, I counter with, 'If you said to me, "I love R. because I want to love R.", I wouldn't be too impressed, and nor would she.' As it is my birthday, T. refrains from throwing his drink over me.

When I return home, I find a small package pushed through the door. My first response is one of mild irritation, as I have specifically requested No Presents, and this particular friend, known for her giftliness, has been warned more than once on the subject. The package contains a lapel badge, battery driven, which flashes '60 TODAY' in blue and red points. What makes it not just acceptable, but the perfect present, turning my irritation into immediate good humour, are the manufacturer's words printed on the cardboard backing: 'WARNING: May Cause Interference With Pacemakers'.

One of the (possibly) 'worthwhile short-term worries' that follows my birthday is an American book tour. The arrival into New York – the transit from airport to city – involves passing one of the vastest cemeteries I have ever seen. I always half-enjoy this ritual memento mori, prob-ably because I have never come to love New York. All the bustle in that most ever-bustling and narcissistic of cities will come to this; Manhattan mocked by the packed verticality of the headstones. In the past, I have merely noted the extent of the graveyards and the arithmetic of mortality. Now, for the first time, something else strikes me: that there is no one in them. These cemeteries are like the modern countryside: hectares of emptiness extending in every direction. And while you hardly expect a yokel with a scythe, a hedger-and-ditcher or a drystone-waller, the utter absence of human activity that agribusiness has brought to the former meadows and pasture-land and hedgerowed fields is another kind of death: as if the pesticides have killed off all the farm workers as well. Similarly, in these Queens cemeteries, not a body – not a soul – stirs. Of course, it makes sense: the dead ex-bustlers are unvisited because the city's new replacement bustlers are much too busy bustling. But if there is anything more melancholy than a graveyard, it is an unvisited graveyard.

A few days later, on the train down to Washington, somewhere south of Trenton, I pass another cemetery. Though equally empty of the living, this one seems less grim: it straggles companionably alongside the tracks, and doesn't have the same feel of stained finality, of dead-and-doneness. Here, it seems, the dead are not so dead that they are forgotten, not so dead that they will not welcome new neighbours. And there, at the southern end of this unmenacing strip, is a cheery American moment: a sign proclaiming BRISTOL CEMETERY – LOTS AVAILABLE.

It reads as if the pun on 'lots' is intended: come and join us, we have much more space than our rivals.

Lots available. Advertise, even in death – it's the American way. Whereas in Western Europe the old religion is in terminal decline, America remains a Christian country, and it makes sense that the creed still flourishes there. Christianity, which cleared up the old Jewish doctrinal dispute about whether or not there was life after death, which centralized personal immortality as a theological selling-point, is well suited to this can-do, reward-driven society. And since in America all tendencies are taken to the extreme, they have currently installed Extreme Christianity. Old Europe took a more leisurely approach to the final arrival of the Kingdom of Heaven – a long mouldering in the grave before resurrection and judgement, all in God's good time. America, and Extreme Christianity, likes to hurry things along. Why shouldn't product delivery follow promised order sooner rather than later? Hence such fantasies as The Rapture, in which the righteous, while going about their daily business, are instantly taken up into Heaven, there to watch Jesus and the Antichrist duke it out down below on the battleground of planet Earth. The action-man, X-rated, disaster-movie version of the world's end.

Death followed by resurrection: the ultimate 'tragedy with a happy ending'. That phrase is routinely credited to one of those Hollywood directors who are assumed to be the source of all witticism; though I first came across it in

Edith Wharton's autobiography *A Backward Glance*. There she ascribes the quip to her friend the novelist William Dean Howells, who offered it her as consolation after a first-night audience had failed to appreciate a theatrical adaptation of *The House of Mirth*. This would take the phrase back to 1906, before all those movie directors had started making wisecracks.

Wharton's success as a novelist is the more surprising – and the more admirable – given how little her view of life accorded with American hopefulness. She saw small evidence of redemption. She thought life a tragedy – or at best a grim comedy – with a tragic ending. Or, sometimes, just a drama with a dramatic ending. (Her friend Henry James defined life as 'a predicament before death'. And *his* friend Turgenev believed that 'the most interesting part of life is death'.)

Nor was Wharton seduced by the notion that life, whether tragic, comic or dramatic, is necessarily original. Our lack of originality is something we usefully forget as we hunch over our – to us – ever-fascinating lives. My friend M., leaving his wife for a younger woman, used to complain, 'People tell me it's a cliché. But it doesn't feel like a cliché to me.' Yet it was, and is. As all our lives would prove, if we could see them from a greater distance – from the viewpoint, say, of that higher creature imagined by Einstein.

A biographer friend once suggested she take the slightly longer view and write my life. Her husband argued satirically that this would make a very short work as all my days were the same. 'Got up,' his version went. 'Wrote book. Went out, bought bottle of wine. Came home, cooked dinner. Drank wine.' I immediately endorsed this Brief Life. That will do as well as any other; as true, or as untrue as anything longer. Faulkner said that a writer's obituary should read: 'He wrote books, and then he died.'

SHOSTAKOVICH KNEW THAT making art from and about death was 'tantamount to wiping your sleeve on your nose'. When the sculptor Ilya Slonim did a portrait bust of him, the result failed to please the chairman of the Soviet Committee for the Arts. 'What we need,' the apparatchik told the sculptor (and by extension the composer), 'is an optimistic Shostakovich.' The composer loved repeating this oxymoron.

Apart from being a great brooder on death, he was also – in private, necessarily – a mocker of false hopes, state propaganda and artistic dross. One favourite target was a hit play of the 1930s by the long-forgotten regime creep Vsevolod Vishnevsky, of whom a Russian theatre scholar recently wrote: 'Even by the standards of our literary herbarium, this author was a very poisonous specimen.' Vishnevsky's play was set on board ship during the Bolshevik Revolution, and admirably portrayed the world as the authorities pretended it was. A young female commissar arrives to explain, and impose, the party line on a crew of anarchist sailors and old-school Russian officers.

She is met with indifference, scepticism, and even assault: one of the sailors tries to rape her, whereupon she shoots him dead. Such an example of communist vigour and instant justice helps win over the sailors, who are soon moulded into an effective fighting unit. Deployed against the warmongering, God-worshipping, capitalistic Germans, they are somehow taken prisoner; but rise up heroically against their captors. During the struggle the inspirational commissar is killed, and dies urging the now fully Sovietized sailors, 'Always uphold ... the high traditions ... of the Red Fleet.' Curtain.

It wasn't the cartoonishly obedient plot of Vishnevsky's play that appealed to Shostakovich's sense of humour, but its title: *An Optimistic Tragedy.* Soviet Communism, Hollywood and organized religion were all closer than they knew, dream factories cranking out the same fantasy. 'Tragedy is tragedy', Shostakovich liked to repeat, 'and optimism has nothing to do with it.'

I HAVE SEEN two dead people, and touched one of them; but I've never seen anyone die, and may never do so, unless and until I see myself die. If death ceased to be talked about when it first really began to be feared, and then more so when we started to live longer, it has also gone off the agenda because it has ceased to be there, with us, in the house. Nowadays we make death as invisible as possible, and part of a process – from doctor to hospital to undertaker to crematorium – in which professionals and bureaucrats tell us what to do, up to the point where we are left to ourselves, survivors standing with a glass in our hands, amateurs learning how to mourn. But not so long ago the dying would have spent their final illness at home, expired among family, been washed and laid out by local women, watched over companionably for a night or two, then coffined up by the local undertaker. Like Jules Renard, we would have set off on foot behind a swaying, horse-drawn hearse for the cemetery, there to watch the coffin being lowered and a fat worm strutting at the grave's edge. We would have been more attending and more attentive. Better for them (though my brother will refer me to hypo-thetical wants of the dead), and probably better for us. The old system made for a statelier progressing from being alive to being dead – and from being dead to being lost from sight. The modern, rushing way is doubtless truer to how we see death nowadays – one minute you're alive, the next you're dead, and truly dead, so let's jump in the car and get it over with. (Whose car shall we take? Not the one she would have wanted.)

Stravinsky went to see Ravel's body before it was placed in the coffin. It was lying on a table draped in black. Every-thing was black and white: black suit, white gloves, white hospital turban still encircling the head, black wrinkles on a very pale face, which had 'an expression of great majesty'. And there the grandeur of death ended. 'I went to the interment,' Stravinsky recorded. 'A lugubrious experience, these civil burials where everything is banned except protocol.' That was Paris, 1937. When Stravinsky's turn came, thirty-four years later, his body was flown from New York to Rome, then driven to Venice, where black and purple proclamations were posted up everywhere: THE CITY OF VENICE DOES HOMAGE TO THE REMAINS OF THE GREAT MUSICIAN IGOR STRAVINSKY, WHO IN A GESTURE OF EXQUISITE FRIENDSHIP ASKED TO BE BURIED IN THE CITY WHICH HE LOVED ABOVE ALL OTHERS. The Archimandrite of Venice conducted the Greek Orthodox service in the church of SS Giovanni et Paolo, then the coffin was carried past the Colleoni statue, and rowed by four gondoliers in a water-hearse out to the cemetery island of San Michele. There the Archimandrite and Stravinsky's widow dropped earth from their hands on to the coffin as it was lowered into the vault. Francis Steegmuller, the great Flaubert scholar, followed the day's events. He said that as the cortège processed from church to canal, with Venetians hanging from every window, the scene resembled 'one of Carpaccio's pageants'. More, much more than protocol.

Unless and until I see myself die. Would you rather be conscious of your dying, or unconscious of it? (There is a third – and highly popular – option: being deluded into the belief that you are on the way to recovery.) But be careful what you wish for. Roy Porter wanted to be fully conscious: 'Because, you know, you'd just be missing out on something otherwise.' He went on: 'Clearly, one doesn't want excruciating pain and all the rest of it. But I think one would want to be with the people who mattered to one.' That is what Porter hoped for, and this is what he got. He was fifty-five, had recently taken early retirement, moved to Sussex with his fifth wife, and begun a life of freelance writing. He was bicycling home from his allotment (hard not to imagine the kind of country lane where Bertrand Russell had his marital aperçu) when he was suddenly blasted out by a heart attack, and died alone on the verge. Did he have any time to watch himself die? Did he know he was dying? Was his last thought an expectation that he would wake up in hospital? His final morning had been spent planting peas. And he was taking home a bunch of flowers, which were in a moment transformed into his own roadside tribute.

MY GRANDFATHER SAID that remorse was the worst emotion life could contain. My mother did not understand the remark, and I do not know what events to attach it to.

Death and Remorse 1. When François Renard, ignoring his son's advice to take an enema, took a shotgun instead, and used a walking stick to fire both barrels and produce a 'dark place above the waist, like a small extinguished fire', Jules wrote: 'I do not reproach myself for not having loved him enough. I reproach myself for not having understood him.'

Death and Remorse 2. Ever since I first read it, I have remained haunted by a line from Edmund Wilson's journals. Wilson died in 1972; the events referred to happened in 1932; I read about them in 1980, the year *The Thirties* was published.

At the beginning of that decade, Wilson had married, as his second wife, one Margaret Canby. She was a stocky, humorous-faced, upper-class woman with 'champagne tastes': Wilson was the first man she had known who had worked for a living. In the previous volume of his journals, *The Twenties*, Wilson had called her 'the best woman drinking companion I had ever known'. There he noted his first intention of marrying her, and also his sensible hesitation: 'Well though we got along, we did not have enough in common.' But marry they did, into an alcoholic companionship marked from the first by infidelity and temporary separations. If Wilson had his doubts about Canby, she had even stronger reservations about him. 'You're a cold fishy leprous person, Bunny Wilson,' she once told him – a remark which Wilson, with typical unsparingness, confided to his diary.

In September 1932 the couple, then married two years, were having one of their separations. Margaret Canby was in California, Wilson in New York. She went to a party in Santa Barbara wearing high heels. As she left, she tripped, fell down a flight of stone steps, broke her skull and died. The event produced, in Wilson's journal, forty-five pages of the most honest and self-flagellant mourning ever written. Wilson starts taking notes as his plane slowly hedge-hops west, as if the enforced literary act will help block off emotion. Over the next days, these jottings open out into an extraordinary monologue of homage, erotic remembrance, remorse and despair. 'A horrible night but even that seemed sweet in recollection,' he notes at one point. In California, Canby's mother urges him: 'You must believe in immortality, Bunny, you must!' But he doesn't and can't: Margaret is dead and unreturning.

Wilson spares himself, and his putative reader, nothing. He preserves every impaling rebuke Canby delivered. She once told her critical, complaining husband that the epitaph on his tombstone should read: 'You'd better go and fix yourself up.' He also celebrates her: in bed, in drink, in tears, in confusion. He remembers fighting off the flies when they made love on a beach, and iconizes her 'cunning' body with its small limbs. ('Don't say that!' she would protest. 'It makes me sound like a turtle.') He calls to mind the ignorances that charmed him — 'I've found out what that thing over the door is – it's a lentil' – and places them alongside her running complaints: 'I'll crash someday! Why don't you do something about me?' She accused him of treating her as just another luxury item, like Guerlain scent: 'You'd be charmed if I were dead, you know you would.'

The fact that Wilson treated his wife badly, both before and after marriage, and that his grief was contaminated by justified guilt, is what gives this stream of mourning consciousness its power. The animating paradox of Wilson's condition is that he has been released into feeling by the death of the person who accused him of lack of feeling. And the line that has never left my memory is this: 'After she was dead, I loved her.'

It doesn't matter that Bunny Wilson was a cold, fishy, leprous person. It doesn't matter that their relationship was a mistake and their marriage a disaster. It only matters that Wilson was telling the truth, and that the authentic voice of remorse is sounded in those words: 'After she was dead, I loved her.'

WE MAY ALWAYS choose knowledge over ignorance; we may wish to be conscious of our dying; we may hope for a best-case scenario in which a calm mind observes a gradual decline, perhaps with a Voltairean finger on the ebbing pulse. We may get all this; but even so, we should consider the evidence of Arthur Koestler. In *Dialogue with Death* he recorded his experiences in the Francoist prisons of Malaga and Seville during the Spanish Civil War. Admittedly, there is a difference between young men facing immediate execution by political opponents, and older men and women, most of their lives behind them, contemplating quieter extinctions. But Koestler observed many of those about to die – including, as he was assured, himself – and came to the following conclusions. First, that no one, even in the condemned cell, even hearing the sound of their friends and comrades being shot, can ever truly believe in his own death; indeed, Koestler thought this fact could be expressed quasi-mathematically – 'One's disbelief in death grows in proportion to its approach.' Secondly, the mind has recourse to various tricks when it finds itself in the presence of death: it produces 'merciful narcotics or ecstatic stimulants' to deceive us. In particular, Koestler thought, it is capable of splitting consciousness in two, so that one half is examining coolly what the other half is experiencing. In this way, 'the consciousness sees to it that its complete annihilation is never experienced'. Two decades previously, in 'Thoughts for the Times on War and Death', Freud had written: 'It is indeed impossible to imagine our own death; and whenever we attempt to do so, we can perceive that we are in fact still present as spectators.'

Koestler also casts doubt on the authenticity of death-bed self-observation, however apparently lucid and rational the mind. 'I don't believe that since the world began a human being has ever died *consciously*. When Socrates, sitting in the midst of his pupils, reached out for the goblet of hemlock, he must have been at least half convinced that he was merely showing off . . . Of course he knew that theoretically the draining of the goblet would prove fatal; but he must have had a feeling that the whole thing was quite different from what his perfervid, humourless pupils imagined it; that there was some clever dodge behind it all known only to himself.'

Koestler ends *Dialogue with Death* with a scene so cinematic, so neat and so implausible that he cannot possibly have made it up. He has been released from prison in exchange for the wife of a Francoist fighter ace, who is given the job of flying Koestler to the rendezvous. As their plane hovers over a vast white plateau, the black-shirted pilot takes his hand off the joystick and engages his political enemy in a shouted conversation about life and death, Left and Right, courage and cowardice. 'Before we were alive,' the writer bellows at the aviator at one point, 'we were all dead.' The pilot agrees, and asks, 'But why, then, is one afraid of death?' 'I have never been afraid of death,' Koestler replies, 'but only of dying.' 'With me, it's exactly the opposite,' shouts back the man in the black shirt.

Except that they were, presumably, shouting in Spanish. Fear of death or fear of dying, would you rather? Are you with the Communist or the Fascist, the writer or the flyer? Almost everyone fears one to the exclusion of the other; it's as if there isn't enough room for the mind to contain both. If you fear death, you don't fear dying; if you fear dying, you don't fear death. But there's no logical reason why one should block out the other; no reason why the mind, with a little training, cannot stretch to encompass both. As one who wouldn't mind dying as long as I didn't end up dead afterwards, I can certainly make a start on elaborating what my fears about dying might be. I fear being my father as he sat in a chair by his hospital bed and with quite uncharacteristic irateness rebuked me – 'You said you were coming *yesterday*' – before working out from my embarrassment that it was he who had got things confused. I fear being my mother imagining that she still played tennis. I fear being the friend who, longing for death, would repeatedly confide that he had managed to acquire and swallow enough pills to kill himself, but was now seethingly anxious that his actions might get a nurse into trouble. I fear being the innately courteous literary man I knew who, as senility took hold, began spouting at his wife the most extreme sexual fantasies, as if they were what he had always secretly wanted to do to her. I fear being the octogenarian Somerset Maugham, dropping his trousers behind the sofa and shitting on the rug (even if the moment might happily recall my childhood). I fear being the elderly friend, a man of both refinement and squeamishness, whose eyes showed animal panic when the nurse in the residential home announced in front of visitors that it was time to change his nappy. I fear the nervous laugh I shall give when I don't quite get an allusion or have forgotten a shared memory, or a familiar face, and then begin to mistrust much of what I think I know, and finally mistrust all of it. I fear the catheter and the stairlift, the oozing body and the wasting brain. I fear the Chabrier/ Ravel fate of not knowing who I have been and what I have made. Perhaps Stravinsky, in extreme old age, had their endings in mind when he used to call out from his room for his wife or a member of the household. 'What is it you need?' they would ask. 'To be reassured of my own existence,' he would reply. And the confirmation might come in the form of a handclasp, a kiss, or the playing of a favourite record.

Arthur Koestler, in old age, was proud of a conundrum he had formulated: 'Is it better for a writer to be forgotten before he dies, or to die before he is forgotten?' (Jules Renard knew his answer: 'Poil de Carotte and I live together, and I hope that I die before him.') But it is a would-you-rather porous enough to allow a third possibility to sneak in: the writer, before dying, may have lost all memory of having been a writer.

When Dodie Smith was asked if she remembered having been a famous playwright, and replied, 'Yes, I *think* so', she said it in exactly the same way – with a kind of frowning concentration, morally conscious that truth was required – as I had seen her answer dozens of questions over the years. In other words, she at least remained in character. Beyond those nearer fears of mental and physical slippage, this is what we hope and hold to for ourselves. We want people to say, 'He was himself right to the end, you know, even if he couldn't speak/see/hear.' Though science and self-knowledge have led us to doubt what our individuality consists of, we still want to remain in that character which we have perhaps deceived ourselves into believing is ours, and ours alone.

Memory is identity. I have believed this since – oh, since I can remember. You are what you have done; what you have done is in your memory; what you remember defines who you are; when you forget your life you cease to be, even before your death. I once spent many years failing to save a friend from a long alcoholic decline. I watched her, from close at hand, lose her short-term memory, and then her long-term, and with them most of everything in between. It was a terrifying example of what Lawrence Durrell in a poem called 'the slow disgracing of the mind': the mind's fall from grace. And with that fall – the loss of specific and general memories being patched over by absurd feats of fabulation, as the mind reassured itself and her but no one else – there was a comparable fall for those who knew and loved her. We were trying to hold on to our memories of her – and thus, quite simply, to her – telling ourselves that 'she' was still there, clouded over but occasionally visible in sudden moments of truth and clarity. Protestingly, I would repeat, in an attempt to convince myself as much as those I was addressing, 'She's just the same underneath.' Later I realized that I had always been fooling myself, and the 'underneath' was being – had been – destroyed at the same rate as the visible surface. She had gone, was off in a world that convinced only herself – except that, from her panic, it was clear that such conviction was only occasional. Identity is memory, I told myself; memory is identity.

DYING IN CHARACTER: an instructive case. Eugene O'Kelly was a fifty-three-year-old chairman and CEO of a top American accountancy firm. By his own description, he was a paradigmatic success story: a 'type A' personality with 20,000 employees under him, a frenetic schedule, children he didn't see enough of, and a devoted wife he referred to as 'my own personal Sherpa'. Here is O'Kelly's account of what he termed 'My Perfect Day':

> I have a couple of face-to-face client meetings, my favourite thing of all. I'd meet with at least one member of my inner team. I'd speak on the phone with partners, in New York and in offices around the country, to see how I could help them. I'd put out some fires. Sometimes I'd have a discussion with one of our competitors about how we could work together towards one of our professional common goals. I'd complete lots of items listed in my electronic calendar. And I'd move ahead in at least one of three areas I'd resolved to improve when I was elected to the top spot by the partners of the firm three years earlier: growing our business . . . enhancing quality and reducing risk; and, most vital to me and the long-term health of the firm, making our firm an even better place to work, indeed a great place to work, one that allowed our people to live more balanced lives.

In the spring of 2005, O'Kelly was 'one of 50 CEOs invited to participate at a White House business round-table with President Bush. Was anyone luckier in his job than I?'

But just at that moment, O'Kelly's luck ran out. What he thought was temporary tiredness after an especially tough schedule turned into a slightly drooping cheek muscle, then into a suspicion of Bell's palsy, and then – suddenly, irreversibly – into a diagnosis of inoperable brain cancer. This was one fire that could not be put out. All the most expensive experts could not divert the onrushing truth: three months and barely a day longer.

O'Kelly responds to this news like the 'goal-driven person' and ultimate corporate competitor that he is. 'Just as a successful executive is driven to be as strategic and prepared as possible to "win" at everything, so I was now driven to be as methodical as possible during my last hundred days.' He plans to apply 'the skill set of a CEO' to his predicament. He realizes that he must 'come up with new goals. Fast.' He tries to 'figure out how I as an individual needed to reposition swiftly to adjust to the new circumstances of my life'. He draws up 'the final and most important to-do list of my life'.

Priorities, methods, targets. He gets his business and financial affairs in order. He decides how he is going to 'unwind' his relationships by creating 'perfect moments' and 'perfect days'. He begins 'transition to the next state'. He plans his own funeral. Ever competitive, he wants to make his death 'the best death possible', and after completing his to-do list, concludes: 'Now, I was motivated to "succeed" at death.'

For those who think that any Hundred Days inevitably

leads to Waterloo, the notion of 'succeeding at death' may seem grotesque, even comic. But then everyone's death will be comic to someone. (Do you know what O'Kelly did shortly after learning that he had only three months to live? He wrote a *short story*! As if the world needed another one . . .) And then, with the help of what must inevitably be called a ghost, he put together the book you decide to write – the one about dying – when faced with your final delivery date.

O'Kelly lists and categorizes the friendships he needs to unwind. Even before he gets to his inner circle there are, astonishingly, a thousand names in his book. But with the speed and attack of one used to closing deals, he completes the job in three weeks flat: sometimes with a note or phone call, occasionally with a brief meeting which might perhaps contain a 'perfect moment'. When it comes to unwinding closer friendships there is some sporadic human resistance. One or two friends don't want to be fobbed off with a single farewell, a stroll round the park while shared memories are evoked. But like a true CEO, O'Kelly overrides such clinging sentimentalists. He says firmly, 'I'd like this to be it. I set this up specifically so we could unwind. And we made a perfect moment out of this. Let's take that and go forward. Let's not schedule another one. Trying to improve on a perfect moment never works.'

No, I don't think I'd put it like that either. But then, I doubt I've met anyone quite like O'Kelly. The 'unwinding' he plans for his teenage daughter involves a trip to Prague,

Rome and Venice. 'We would fly by private jet, which would require us to refuel somewhere in the far, far north, and that would give Gina an opportunity to meet and trade with the Inuits.' This is not so much dying in character as dying in caricature. You say goodbye to your daughter, but you also build in for her *an opportunity to trade with the Inuits*? And do you inform the Inuits what their privileged function is to be on this occasion?

Such moments may provoke a satirical and disbelieving gawp. But O'Kelly was surely dying as he had lived, and we should all be so lucky. Whether or not he cheated a little is another matter. The CEO had not previously had much truck with God, because of the tightness of his schedule; though he did use Him as a kind of emergency break-down service. Some years previously, the prospective Inuit-trader had been diagnosed with juvenile arthritis, and her father remembered that 'You could find me in church often that year.' Now, with his own final deal shortly to be closed, O'Kelly again refers things upwards, to the transnational HQ in the sky. He prays, and learns to meditate. He feels supported from 'the other side' and reports that 'there is no pain between this side and the other side'. His wife explains that 'If you conquer fear, you conquer death' – though you don't, of course, end up *not dead*. When O'Kelly expires it is, according to his own personal Sherpa, 'in a state of tranquil acceptance and genuine hope'.

Psychoanalysts tell us that those who are most attached

to their own personalities have the most difficulty in dying. Given O'Kelly's A-typeness, his age, and the swiftness of his end, his behaviour is highly impressive. And perhaps God doesn't mind being addressed only in emergency. It may seem to bystanders that any sensible deity ought to be offended by such spotty, self-interested attention. But He might view things differently. He might, modestly, not want to be a daily, occluding presence in our lives. He might enjoy being a breakdown specialist, an insurance company, a longstop.

O'Kelly didn't want organ music at his funeral; he specified flute and harp. I gave my mother Mozart; she gave my father Bach. We spend time thinking about our funeral music; less about what music we wish to do our dying with. I remember the literary editor Terence Kilmartin, one of my early encouragers, lying on a bed downstairs when he was too weak to climb a stair, listening to late Beethoven string quartets on a portable boom box. Dying popes and emperors could summon their own choirs and instrumentalists to help them sample the glory to come. But modern technology has made popes and emperors of us all; and though you may reject the Christian heaven, you can have the Bach *Magnificat*, Mozart's *Requiem* or Pergolesi's *Stabat Mater* lighting up the inside of your skull as your body fades. Sydney Smith thought of heaven as eating foie gras to the sound of trumpets – which has always felt to me like a clash rather than a concord. Still, you could have the rousing massed brass of Gounod's *St Cecilia Mass* thundering in your ears while a tube bubbles sugary feed into your arm.

I suspect that if I get any sort of decent dying time, I shall want music rather than books. Will there be space – head-space – for the wonderful trudgery of fiction, the work involved: plot, characters, situation . . . ? No, I think I'm going to need music, fittingly intravenous: straight to the bloodstream, straight to the heart. 'The best means we have of digesting time' will perhaps help us digest the beginnings of death. Music is also associated for me with optimism. I had an instant sense of fellow-feeling when I read that one of the pleasures of Isaiah Berlin's old age was booking concert tickets for months ahead (I often used to spot him, up in the same box at the Festival Hall). Getting the tickets somehow guarantees that you will hear the music, prolongs your life at least until the last echo of the final chords you have paid to hear dies away. Somehow, this wouldn't work with the theatre.

It would, however, depend upon successfully remaining in character. When first considering my best-case death scenario (x months, time for 200–250 pages), I took this matter for granted. I assumed that I would remain myself to the end, also instinctively insist on being a writer, keen to describe and define the world even as I was leaving it. But the character may be subjected to sudden jolts, magnifications and distortions in its final stages. A friend of Bruce Chatwin's first realized that the writer must be seriously ill when he paid for lunch, an action hitherto quite

I suspect that if I get any sort of decent dying time, I shall want music rather than books untypical of him. Who can predict the mind's response to its own short-dated termination?

'WE SHALL PROBABLY die in hospital, you and I.' A foolish thing to write, however statistically probable. The pace, as well as the place, of our dying is fortunately hidden from us. Expect one thing and you will likely get another. On 21 February 1908, Jules Renard wrote: 'Tomorrow I shall be forty-four. It's not much of an age. Forty-five is when you have to start thinking. Forty-four is a year lived upon velvet.' On his actual birthday, he was a little more sombre: 'Forty-four – the sort of age at which you must give up hope of ever doubling your years.'

To admit that you might not make it to eighty-eight seems a modest calculation rather than a declaration of defiance. Even so, by the following year, Renard's health had declined so sharply that he was unable to walk from one end of the Tuileries to the other without sitting down for a chat with the old women selling lilies of the valley. 'I shall have to start taking notes on my old age,' he concluded, and wrote ruefully to a friend, 'I'm forty-five – that wouldn't be old if I were a tree.' Once, he had asked God not to let him die too quickly, as he wouldn't mind observing the process. How much observation did he now think he would need? He made it to forty-six and three months.

When his mother fell backwards into the well, creating 'the soft eddy familiar to those who have drowned an animal', Renard commented, 'Death is not an artist.' Its virtues are at best artisanal: diligence, stubborn application and a sense of contradictoriness which at times rises to the level of irony; but it doesn't have enough subtlety, or ambiguity, and is more repetitive than a Bruckner symphony. True, it has complete flexibility of location, and a pretty array of encircling customs and superstitions – though these are our doing, rather than its. Renard noted one detail certainly unknown to my folklorically impoverished family: 'As death approaches, one smells of fish.' Now that's something to look out for.

Though why should Death care if we join Renard in snootily excluding it from the guild of artists? When has it ever looked for Art's approval? With its co-worker Time, it just goes about its business, a cheerless commissar reliably fulfilling a quota of one hundred per cent. Most artists keep a wary eye on death. Some see it as a hurry-up call; some optimistically trust that posterity's hindsight will bring their vindication (though 'Why should people be less stupid tomorrow than they are today?'); for others, death is the best career move. Shostakovich, noting that the fear of death is probably the deepest feeling we have, went on: 'The irony lies in the fact that under the influence of that fear people create poetry, prose and music; that is, they try to strengthen their ties with the living and increase their influence on them.'

Do we create art in order to defeat, or at least defy, death? To transcend it, to put it in its place? You may take my body, you may take all the squidgy stuff inside my skull where lurks whatever lucidity and imagination I possess, but you cannot take away what I have done with them. Is that our subtext and our motivation? Most probably – though *sub specie aeternitatis* (or even the view of a millennium or two) it's pretty daft. '*Les dieux eux-mêmes meurent. | Mais les vers souverains | Demeurent | Plus forts que les airains.*' [The Gods themselves die out, but Poetry, stronger even than bronze, survives everything.] Those proud lines of Gautier's I was once so attached to as a student – everything passes, except art in its robustness; kings die, but sovereign poetry lasts longer than bronze – now read as adolescent consolation. Tastes change; truths become clichés; whole art forms disappear. Even the greatest art's triumph over death is risibly temporary. A novelist might hope for another generation of readers – two or three if lucky – which may feel like a scorning of death; but it's really just scratching on the wall of the condemned cell. We do it to say: I was here too.

WE MAY ALLOW Death, like God, to be an occasional ironist, but shouldn't nevertheless confuse them. The essential difference remains: God might be dead, but Death is well alive.

Death as ironist: the *locus classicus* is the 1000-year-old story I first came across when reading Somerset Maugham. A merchant in Baghdad sends his servant out to buy provisions. In the market the man is jostled by a woman; turning, he recognizes her as Death. He runs home pale and trembling, and pleads for the loan of his master's horse: he must go at once to Samarra and hide where Death will never find him. The master agrees; the servant rides off. The master himself then goes down to the market, accosts Death and rebukes her for threatening his servant. Oh, replies Death, but I made no threatening gesture – that was just surprise. I was startled to see the fellow in Baghdad this morning, given that I have an appointment with him in Samarra tonight.

And here is a more modern story. Pavel Apostolov was a musicologist, composer for brass band, and lifelong persecutor of Shostakovich. During the Great Patriotic War he had been a colonel commanding a regiment; afterwards, he became a key member of the Central Committee's music section. Shostakovich said of him: 'He rode in on a white horse, and did away with music.' In 1948, Apostolov's committee forced the composer to recant his musical sins, and drove him close to suicide.

Twenty years later, Shostakovich's death-haunted 14th Symphony was given a 'closed premiere' in the Small Hall of the Moscow Conservatoire. This was in effect a private vetting by Soviet musical experts, with no danger of the new work infecting the greater public. Before the concert Shostakovich addressed the audience. The violinist Mark Lubotsky remembered him saying: 'Death is terrifying, there is nothing beyond it. I don't believe in life beyond the grave.' Then he asked the audience to be as quiet as possible because the performance was being recorded.

Lubotsky was sitting next to a female administrator of the Composers' House; beyond her was an elderly, bald man. The symphony had reached its intensely quiet fifth movement when the man jumped up, banged his seat loudly, and rushed out of the hall. The administrator whispered, 'What a bastard! He tried to destroy Shostakovich in 1948, but failed. He still hasn't given up, and he's gone and wrecked the recording on purpose.' It was, of course, Apostolov. What those present didn't realize, however, was that the wrecker was himself being wrecked – by a heart attack which was to prove fatal. The 'sinister symphony of death', as Lubotsky called it, was in fact grimly playing him out.

The Samarra story shows how we used to think of death: as a stalker on the prowl, watching and waiting to strike; a black-clad figure with scythe and hourglass; something out there, personifiable. The Moscow story shows death as it normally is: what we bear within us all the time, in some piece of potentially berserk genetic material, in some flawed organ, in the time-stamped machinery of which we are made up. When we lie on that deathbed, we may well go back to personifying death, and think we are fighting illness as if it were an invader; but we shall really just be fighting ourselves, the bits of us that want to kill the rest of us. Towards the end – if we live long enough – there is often a competition among our declining and decaying parts as to which will get top billing on our death certificate. As Flaubert put it, 'No sooner do we come into this world than bits of us start dropping off.'

The bit of Jules Renard that did for him was his heart. He was diagnosed with emphysema and arteriosclerosis, and began his last year *au lit et au lait* (bed and milk – two and a half litres a day). He said: 'Now that I am ill, I find I want to make some profound and historic utterances, which my friends will subsequently repeat; but then I get too over-excited.' He teasingly gave his sister responsibility for having his bust erected in the little square in Chitry-les-Mines. He said that writers had a better, truer sense of reality than doctors. He felt his heart was behaving like a buried miner, knocking at irregular intervals to signal that it was still alive. He felt that parts of his brain were being blown away like a dandelion clock. He said: 'Don't worry! Those of us who fear death always try to die as stylishly as possible.' He said: 'Paradise does not exist, but we must nonetheless strive to be worthy of it.' The end came in Paris, on 22 May 1910; he was buried at Chitry four days later, without benefit of clergy, like his father and brother before him. At his writerly request, no words were spoken over his body.

Too many French deaths? Very well, here's a good old British death, that of our national connoisseur of mortal terror, Philip Larkin. In the first decades of his life, Larkin could sometimes persuade himself that extinction, when it eventually came, might prove a mercy. But by his fifties, his biographer tells us, 'The dread of oblivion darkened everything' – and then, 'As he entered his sixties his fears grew rapidly.' So much for my friend G.'s reassurance that things get better after sixty. In the year that was to contain his death, Larkin wrote to a fellow poet, 'I don't think about death *all* the time, though I don't see why one shouldn't, just as you might expect a man in a condemned cell to think about the drop all the time. Why aren't I screaming?' he wondered, referring back to his poem 'The Old Fools'.

Larkin died in hospital in Hull. A friend, visiting him the day before, said, 'If Philip hadn't been drugged, he would have been raving. He was that frightened.' At 1.24 a.m., a typical deathing hour, he said his last words, to a nurse holding his hand: 'I am going to the inevitable.' Larkin was hardly a Francophile (though more cosmopolitan than he affected); but you could, if you wished, take this as an allusion to, and correction of, Rabelais' supposed deathbed utterance: 'I am going to seek a Great Perhaps.'

Larkin's death can do nothing but chill. Pit-gazing led not to calm, but to increased terror; and though he feared death, he did not die stylishly. Did Renard? Given the discretion of French biography, there are no specific details; however, one friend, Alphonse Daudet's son Léon, wrote that he showed 'wonderful courage' in his last illness. Daudet concluded: 'Good writers, like good soldiers, know how to die, whereas politicians and doctors are afraid of death. Everyone can corroborate this remark by looking around them. Though there are, of course, exceptions.'

Here is the old argument, as phrased by Renard when he was young and in good health: 'Death is sweet; it delivers us from the fear of death.' Is this not a comfort? No, it is a sophistry. Or rather, further proof that it will take more than logic, and rational argument, to defeat death and its terrors.

AFTER WE DIE, the hair and the fingernails continue spookily to grow for a while. We all know that. I've always believed it, or half-believed it, or half-assumed there must be 'something in it': not that we turn into shock-heads with vampiric fingernails as we lie in our coffins, but, well, perhaps a millimetre or two of hair and nail. Yet what 'we all know' is usually wrong, in part if not whole. As the friendly thanatologist Dr Sherwin Nuland points out, the matter is simple and incontrovertible. When we die, we stop breathing; no air, no blood; no blood, no possible growth. There might be a brief flicker of brain activity after the heart ceases to beat; but that's all. Perhaps this particular myth springs from our fear of live burial. Or perhaps it's based on honest misobservation. If the body appears to shrink – indeed, does shrink – after death, then the flesh of the fingers might pull back, giving the illusion of nail growth; while if the face looks smaller, this might have the effect of giving you bigger hair.

Being wrong: my brother in error. After our mother's death, he took our parents' ashes to the Atlantic coast of France, where they had often holidayed. He and his wife scattered them on the dunes with the help of J., our parents' closest French friend. They read 'Fear no more the heat o' the sun' from *Cymbeline* ('Golden lads and girls all must / As chimney-sweepers, come to dust') and Jacques Prévert's poem *'Les Escargots qui vont à l'enterrement'*; my brother pronounced himself 'strangely moved' by the event. Later, over dinner, conversation turned to our parents' annual visits to that part of France. 'I remember being staggered,' my brother told me, 'when J. described how every night Father had kept them up to the early hours with his anecdotes and lively conversation. I can't remember him ever speaking after they moved to that frightful bungalow, and I had imagined that he had forgotten how to be amusing. But evidently I was quite mistaken.' The best explanation I can offer is that our father's French, being superior to our mother's, enabled him for those few weeks of the year to gain linguistic and social primacy; either that, or our mother, when abroad, might deliberately have become a more conventionally listening wife (however unlikely that sounds).

Being wrong: an error of my own in return. I was breast-fed, my brother bottle-fed: from this I once deduced the bifurcation of our natures. But one of my last visits to my mother produced an uncharacteristic moment of near-intimacy. There had been a report in the newspapers concluding that breastfed children were more intelligent than bottle-fed ones. 'I read that as well,' said Ma, 'and I laughed. Nothing wrong with *my two*, I thought.' And then – under cross-examination – she confirmed that I had no more been breastfed than my brother. I didn't ask her reason: whether a determination to give us an equal start in life, or a squeamishness at a potentially messy business ('Mucky pup!'). Except that it was still not exactly the same start, for she mentioned that we had been fed on different formulae. She even told me the names on the bottles, which I promptly forgot. A theory of temperament based on different brands of commercial baby-milk? That would be pretty tendentious, even I would admit. And nowadays I don't consider my brother's bringing of tea to our mother's sickbed any less warm-hearted than my own self-indulgent (and perhaps lazy) blanket-snuggling.

And here is a more complicated error, if equally long-term. In the early 1950s one of my father's French *assistants*, P., came to us for a few nights until he could find lodgings, and ended up staying the whole year. He was from Corsica, an easy-going fellow with what seemed to my parents the typically Gallic trait of blowing his month's salary as soon as it arrived. He also had an artistic streak: he used to make railway stations out of cornflakes packets, and once gave my parents – perhaps in lieu of rent – two small landscapes he had painted. They hung on the wall throughout my childhood, and struck me as unimaginably skilful; but then, anything remotely representational would have done so. They had a rather dark, Dutch feel to them: one showed a tumbledown bridge across a river, with foliage cascading from the parapet; the other, a windmill against a rowdy sky with three white-headdressed women picnicking in the foreground. You could tell they were artistically done because of the thick brushstrokes used in river, sky and meadow. During my childhood and adolescence, these two paintings hung in the sitting room; later, at the 'frightful bungalow', they presided over the dining table. I must have glanced at them regularly for fifty years and more, without ever asking myself, or my parents, where exactly P. had set up his box of oils. France – his native Corsica, perhaps – Holland, England?

When I was house-clearing after my mother's death, I found in a drawer two postcards showing exactly the same two views. My first instinct was to assume that they had been specially printed for P. to advertise his work: he always had a beretful of theoretically money-making schemes. Then I turned them over and realized that they were commercially produced art cards of typically Breton scenes: 'Vieux Moulin à Cléden' and 'Le Pont fleuri'. What I had all my life imagined to be competent originality was merely competent copying. And then there was a further twist. The cards were signed 'Yvon' in the bottom right-hand corner, as if by the artist. But 'Yvon' turned out to be the name of the card company. So the pictures had been produced in the first place solely in order to be turned into postcards – whereupon P. had turned them back into the 'original' paintings they had never been. A French theorist would have been delighted by all this. I hastened to tell my brother of our fifty-year error, expecting him to be equally amused. He wasn't at all: for the simple reason that he had a clear memory of P. painting the pictures, 'and of thinking how much cleverer it was to copy than to make something up out of your own head'.

Such factual corrections are easily made, and may even feel mentally refreshing. It will be harder to face error about perceptions and judgements you have come to look upon as your own achievements. Take death. For most of my sentient life I've known the vivid dread, and also felt fully able – despite what Freud maintained – to imagine my own eternal non-existence. But what if I am quite wrong? Freud's contention, after all, was that our unconscious mind remains doggedly convinced of our immortality – a thesis irrefutable by its very nature. So perhaps what I think of as pit-gazing is only the illusion of truth-examination because deep down I do not – cannot – believe in the pit; and this illusion may even continue until the very end if Koestler is right about our consciousness splitting when we are *in extremis.*

And there's another way of being wrong: what if the dread we feel in advance – which seems to us so absolute – turns out to be as nothing compared to the real thing? What if our void-imaginings are but the palest rehearsal for what we experience in the final hours? And what, further, if the approach of death overwhelms all known language, so that we cannot even report the truth? A sense of having been wrong all the time: well, Flaubert did say that contradiction is the thing that keeps sanity in place.

And beyond death, God. If there were a games-playing God, He would surely get especial ludic pleasure from disappointing those philosophers who had convinced themselves and others of His non-existence. A. J. Ayer assures Somerset Maugham that there is nothing, and nothingness, after death: whereupon they both find themselves players in God's little end-of-the-pier entertainment called Watch the Fury of the Resurrected Atheist. That's a neat would-you-rather for the God-denying philosopher: would you rather there was nothing after death, and you were proved right, or that there was a wonderful surprise, and your professional reputation was destroyed?

'Atheism is aristocratic,' Robespierre declared. The great twentieth-century British embodiment of this was Bertrand Russell – helped, no doubt, by the fact that he *was* aristocratic. In old age, with his unruly white hair, Russell looked, and was treated, like a wise man halfway to god-head: a one-man *Any Questions?* panel in himself. His disbelief never wavered, and friendly provocateurs took to asking him how he would react if, after a lifetime of propagandizing atheism, he turned out to be wrong. What if the pearly gates were neither a metaphor nor a fantasy, and he found himself faced by a deity he had always denied? 'Well,' Russell used to reply, 'I would go up to Him, and I would say, "You didn't give us enough evidence".'

WHEN I REMEMBER my father, I often think of how his nails used to curve over the flesh of his fingertips. In the weeks after his cremation, I used to imagine, not his face or his bones in the furnace, but those familiar fingernails. Beyond that, I think of the various insults his body showed towards the end. A stroke-damaged brain and tongue; a long scar up his belly which he offered to show me once but I lacked the guts to see; spreading bruises on the backs of his hands from the insertion of drips. Unless we are very lucky, our bodies will reveal the history of our dying. One small revenge might be to die and show no signs of having died. Jules Renard's mother was pulled from the well without a scratch or a scar on her. Not that Death – the ultimate bean counter – would care one way or the other. Any more than it cares whether or not we die in character.

We live, we die, we are remembered, we are forgotten. Not immediately, but in tranches. We remember our parents through most of their adult lives; our grandparents through their last third; beyond that, perhaps, lies a great-grandfather with a scratchy beard and a rank odour. Perhaps he smelt of fish. And beyond that? Photographs, and a little haphazard documentation. In the future generations of ancestors will survive on film and tape and disc, moving, talking, smiling, proving that they too were here. As an adolescent I once hid a tape recorder under the table during dinner in an attempt to prove that, far from it being the 'social event' my mother decreed every meal should be, no one ever said anything remotely interesting and I should therefore be excused conversation and allowed to read a book if I preferred. I did not explain these personal aims, thinking they would become self-evident once the clatter of cutlery, banalities and non sequiturs was played back. Annoyingly, my mother was enchanted by the tape, declaring that we all sounded just like a Pinter play (to my mind a mixed compliment, in both directions). And then we continued exactly as before; and I never kept the tape, so that my parents' voices are quite extinct in the world and play now only in my head.

I see (and hear) my mother in hospital, wearing a green dress, sitting canted over in a wheelchair by her bed. She was cross with me that day: not over tennis, but because I had been asked to discuss her treatment with the doctor. She resented every manifestation of incapacity, just as she resented the futile optimism of physiotherapists. When asked to name the hands on a watch, she declined; when instructed to open or close her eyes, she remained impassive. The doctors were unable to decide if it was a case of couldn't or wouldn't. My assumption was 'wouldn't' – that she was, in lawyer's terminology, 'mute of malice' – because in my company she was able to articulate whole sentences. Painfully – but then the sentences themselves were often filled with pain. For instance: 'You don't understand how difficult it is for a woman who has always controlled her life to be restricted like this.'

I spent some awkward minutes with her that afternoon, then went to find the doctor. His prognosis was very discouraging. As I returned to the ward, I told myself that my face must not betray his professional judgement that the next stroke would almost certainly kill her. But my mother was way ahead of me. Turning a corner, I saw, from twenty yards or more across a crowded ward, that she was beadily alert for my return; and as I progressed towards her, refining the semi-lie that I was about to tell, she stuck out her sole working forearm and delivered a thumbs-down sign. It was the most shocking thing I ever saw her do; the most admirable too, and the one occasion when she tore at my heart.

She thought the hospital ought to amputate her 'useless' arm; she thought, for some time, that she was in France, and wondered how I had found her; she thought a Spanish nurse came from her Oxfordshire village, and that all the other nurses came from the various parts of England where she had lived in the previous eighty years. She thought it 'stupid' not to have expired in a single go. When she asked, 'Do you have any trouble comprehending me?' she pronounced each syllable of the verb fastidiously. 'No, Ma,' I replied, 'I understand everything you say, but you don't always get things completely right.' '*Ha,*' she retorted, as if I were some smiley physio. 'That's putting it mildly. I'm quite *loopy.*'

Her mixture of wild confabulation and lucid insight was constantly wrong-footing. In general, she seemed serene about whether she was visited or not, and took to saying, 'You must go now,' which was the complete bloody opposite of how she had been for decades. One day I looked down at her fingernails. You could see how long it was since she had been able to do them; the heavily lacquered and lovingly shaped nails had continued to grow, pushing on to create an eighth of an inch of clear unvarnished whiteness below the cuticle. The nails she had once imagined herself still tending even if sunk in deafness. I looked upwards from the cuticles: the fingers of her dead arm had now swollen to the size, and to the outer texture, of carrots.

Driving back to London, the setting sun in my mirror, the Haffner Symphony on the radio, I thought: if this is what it's like for someone who has worked with her brain all her life, and can afford decent care, I don't want it. Then wondered if I was deluding myself, and would want it, when it came, on any terms; or whether I would have the courage or the cunning to circumvent it; or whether it just happens, and by happening condemns you to see it through, ragingly, dreadingly. However much you escape your parents in life, they are likely to reclaim you in death – in the manner of your death. The novelist Mary Wesley wrote: 'My family has a propensity – it must be our genes – for dropping dead. Here one minute, gone the next. Neat. I pray that I have inherited this gene. I have no wish to linger, to become a bed-bound bore. A short sharp shock for my loved ones is what I want: nicer for them, lovely for me.'

This is a commonly expressed hope, but one my GP disapproves of. Citing this passage, she calls it 'perhaps another manifestation of the contemporary denial of death', and an attitude that 'attaches no value to the opportunities provided by a final illness'. I don't think either of my parents would have thought of their final illnesses as providing 'opportunities': for sharing memories, saying farewell, expressing remorse or forgiveness; while the funeral-planning – that's to say, their desire for an inexpensive and virtually mourner-free cremation – had been stated some time before. Would my parents have 'succeeded at death' if they had become emotional, confessional, soppy? Would they have found out that this was what they had always wanted? I rather doubt it. Though I regret my father never told me he loved me, I'm pretty sure that he did or had, and his melancholy silence on this and other key matters at least meant that he died in character.

When my mother was first in hospital, there was a comatose old woman in the next bed. She lay on her back, quite unmoving. One afternoon, with my mother in a fairly loopy state of mind, the woman's husband arrived. He was a small, neat, respectable working man, probably in his late sixties. 'Hello, Dulcie, it's Albert,' he announced in a ward-filling voice, with a rich, pure Oxfordshire accent which should have been recorded before it died out. 'Hello my darling, hello my love, are you going to wake up for me?' He kissed her echoingly. 'It's Albert, darling, are you going to wake up for me?' Then: 'I'll just turn you so I can put your hearing aid in.' A nurse arrived. 'I'm putting her hearing aid in. She didn't wake up for me this morning. Oh, it's fallen out. There, I'm going to turn you some more.

Hello darling, hello Dulcie, hello my beautiful, it's Albert, are you going to wake up for me?' And so on, at intervals, for the next quarter of an hour, with a brief break of, 'You said something, didn't you, I know you said something, what did you say?' Then back to 'Hello darling, it's Albert, are you going to wake up for me?' interspersed with more kissing. It pierced the heart (and the head), and was only bearable by its edge of black comedy. My mother and I naturally pretended that nothing was going on, or if it was, nothing that we could hear; though the fact that my father's name had also been Albert was not, I suspect, lost on her.

The fingernails on my mother's useless arm continued to grow at exactly the same rate as the fingernails on the one with which she gave herself the thumbs-down; then she died and, contrary to popular belief, all ten nails stopped growing immediately. As had my father's, which curled round and over the flesh of his finger-pads. My brother's nails (and teeth) have always been stronger than mine, a detail I used to put down to the fact that he is shorter than me, and therefore his calcium is more concentrated. This may be scientific nonsense (and the answer lie in differing brands of commercial baby-milk). In any case, I have thinned my fingernails over the years by running them between my front teeth, automatically, when I am reading, writing, worrying, correcting this very sentence. Perhaps I should stop and find out if they will grow curvingly over my fingertips as my father comes to reclaim me.

MY GRANDFATHER, BERT Scoltock, had only two jokes in his repertoire. The first referred to his and Grandma's wedding day, 4 August 1914, and so came with half a century of repetition (rather than honing): 'We were married the day war broke out,' (heavy pause) 'and it's been *war ever since*!!!' The second was a story drawn out as long as possible, about a chap who went into a café and asked for a sausage roll. He took a bite, then complained that there wasn't any sausage in it. 'You haven't reached it yet,' said the café's proprietor. The fellow took another mouthful and repeated his complaint. 'You've bitten right past it,' came the reply – a punchline my grandfather would then reprise.

My brother agrees that Grandpa was humourless; though when I add 'boring and a little frightening', he dissents. But then Grandpa did favour his first-born grandchild, and taught him how to sharpen a chisel. His was a headmasterly presence in the family, and I can easily summon up his disapproval. For instance: every year, he and Grandma would come over for Christmas. Once, in the early sixties, Grandpa, looking for something to read, went to the bookshelves in my bedroom and, without asking, removed my copy of *Lolita*. I can see the Corgi paperback now, see how my grandfather's woodworking and gardening hands methodically broke the spine as he read. This was something I remember my old school friend Alex Brilliant also used to do – though Alex behaved as if breaking a book's spine showed you were engaging intellectually with its contents; whereas Grandpa's (exactly similar) behaviour seemed to indicate disrespect for both the novel and its author. At every page – from 'fire of my loins' to 'the age when lads / Play with erector sets' – I expected him to throw it down in disgust. Amazingly, he didn't. He had started, so he would finish: English puritanism kept him doggedly ploughing through this Russian tale of American depravity. As I nervously watched him, I began to feel almost as if I had written the novel, and now stood revealed as a secret nymphet-groper. What *could* he be making of it? Eventually, he handed the book back to me, its spine a vertical mess of whitened cicatrices, with the comment, 'It may be *good literature*, but I thought it was SMUTTY.'

At the time, I smirked to myself, as any aesthete going up to Oxford would. But I did my grandfather a disservice. For he had accurately recognized *Lolita*'s appeal to me then: as a vital combination of literature and smut. (There was such a dearth of sexual information – let alone experience – around that a reworking of Renard obtained: 'It is when faced with sex that we turn most bookish.') I also did Grandpa a disservice by suggesting that he left me nothing in his will. Wrong again. My brother corrects me: 'When Grandpa died, he left me his repro Chippendale desk (which I never liked) and he left you his gold half-hunter watch (which I had always coveted).'

An old press cutting in my archive drawer confirms that the desk was a retirement present in 1949, when Bert Scoltock, then sixty, left Madeley Modern Secondary School after thirty-six years as a head teacher in various parts of Shropshire. He also received an armchair – quite probably that very Parker Knoll; also, a fountain pen, a cigarette lighter, and a set of gold cufflinks. Girls from the Domestic Science Centre baked him a two-tier cake; while Eric Frost, 'representing a group of boys from the Woodwork Centre', gave him 'a nut bowl and mallet'. I remember this last item well since it was always on display at my grandparents' bungalow, yet never used. When it finally came into my possession, I understood why: it was comically impractical, the mallet firing shell-shrapnel all over the room while reducing the nuts to powder. I always assumed that Grandpa must have made it himself, since almost every wooden object in house and garden, from trug to book trough to grandmother clock case, had been sawn and sanded and chamfered and dowelled by his own hands. He had a great respect for wood, which he took to its final conclusion. Shocked by the notion that coffins crafted from fine oak and elm were reduced to ashes a day or two later, he specified that his own be made from deal.

As for the gold half-hunter, it has been in my top desk drawer for decades. It comes with a gold fob-chain for waistcoat-wear and a leather strap if you prefer to dangle it from lapel buttonhole into top pocket. I open its back: 'Presented to Mr B. Scoltock, by Managers, Teachers, Scholars and Friends, after his leaving after 18 years as head teacher at Bayston Hill C of E School. June 30th 1931.' I had no idea my brother had ever coveted it, so I tell him that now, after forty-odd years of suffering this sinful emotion, the watch is his. 'As for the half-hunter,' he replies, 'I think he would have wanted you to keep it.' He *would have wanted*? My brother is winding me up with this hypothetical want of the dead. He goes on: 'More to the point, I now want you to keep it.' Yes, indeed, we can only do what *we* want.

I apply to my brother on the subject of Grandpa and Remorse. His explanation is this: 'When he used to tell me stories [about the First World War] they would run up to the time the boat left for France, and then start back again in hospital in England. He never said a word to me about the war. I suppose he was in the trenches. He didn't win any medals, I'm sure, nor was he wounded (not even a blighty). So he must have been invalided out for trench feet? Shell shock? Something less than heroic, in any case. Did he let his chums down? I once thought I'd try to find out what he actually did in the war – no doubt there are regimental records, etc. etc.; but of course I never got round to doing anything.'

In my archive drawer are Grandpa's birth certificate, his marriage certificate, and his photo album – a red cloth-bound book titled 'Scenes from Highways & Byways'. It covers the period 1912 to 1917, after which, it seems, he laid down his camera. Here is Grandpa astride a motorbike in 1912, with Grandma perched on the back; roguishly laying his head on her bosom the following year, while grasping her knee with his hand. Here he is on his wedding day, hand around his bride's shoulder and pipe cocked in front of his white waistcoat, as Europe prepares to blow itself apart; on his honeymoon (a studio shot which has faded less); and with 'Babs' – as my mother was known before becoming Kathleen Mabel – born ten months after the wedding. There are pictures of him on home leave, first with two stripes up – Prestatyn, August 1916 – and finally three. By this time Sergeant Scoltock is in the Grata Quies hospital outside Bournemouth, where he and the other inmates look remarkably perky as they pose in fancy dress for a concert party. Here is my grandfather in blackface, first with a certain Decker (cross-dressing as a nurse), and then with Fullwood (a Pierrot). And here is a sudden deface-ment, a head-shot of a woman, dated in pencil Sept 1915, but with the name (or perhaps the place) erased, and the face so scarred and gouged that only the lips and the Weetabixy hair remain. An obliteration that makes her more intri-guing than 'Nurse Glynn', or even 'Sgt P. Hyde Killed in Action, Dec 1915'. An obliteration which seems to me a much better symbol of death than the ubiquitous skull. You only get down to bone after rotting through time; and when you do, one skull is much like another. Fine as a long-term symbol, but for the action of death itself, try just such a torn, gouged photograph: it looks both personal and instantly, utterly destructive, a ripping away of the light from the eye and the life from the cheek.

Formal investigation of my grandfather's war service is initially hampered by not knowing his regiment or date of enlistment. The first Scoltock to turn up is a box-maker invalided out with a medical statement that reads simply: 'Idiot'. (Oh to have an officially designated Idiot in the family.) But then here comes Private Bert Scoltock of the 17th Battalion, Lancashire Fusiliers, who enlisted on 20 November 1915, and two months later took that boat for France with the 104th Infantry Brigade, 35th Division.

My brother and I are surprised that Grandpa joined up so late. I had always imagined him getting fitted out in khaki just as Grandma was falling pregnant. But this must be a piece of back-imagining from our parents' lives: my father joined up and was sent out to India in 1942, leaving my mother pregnant with what turned out to be my brother. Did Grandpa not volunteer until November 1915 because of his daughter coming into the world? He was, as the inscription on his half-hunter confirms, then head teacher at a Church of England school, so perhaps he was in a reserved profession. Or did such a category not yet exist, given that conscription wasn't introduced until January 1916? Perhaps he saw it coming and preferred to volunteer. If Grandma was already a socialist by this time, he might have wanted to show that, despite having a politically suspicious wife, he was nonetheless patriotic. Did one of those smug women come up to him in the street and offer him a white feather? Did he have a close chum who joined up? Was he suffering from a recently married man's fear of entrapment? Is all this absurdly fanciful? Perhaps trying to trace his statement about remorse back to the First World War is misconceived, since it never came with any date attached. I once asked my mother why Grandpa never talked about the war. She replied, 'I don't think he thought it was very interesting.'

Grandpa's personal records (like those of many others) were destroyed by enemy action during the Second World War. The brigade diary shows that they reached the Western Front in late January 1916; there was heavy rain; Kitchener inspected them on 11 February 1916. In July, they finally saw action (casualties 19th–27th: 8 officers wounded; Other Ranks, 34 killed, 172 wounded). The following month, the brigade was in Vaux, Montagne, and the front line at Montauban; Grandpa would have been in Dublin Trench, where the brigade complained of being shelled by their own under-aiming artillery; later in Chimpanzee Trench, at the south end of Angle Wood. In September and October they were in the line again (4th Sept–31st Oct, Other Ranks Casualties: 1 killed, 14 wounded – 3 accidental, 3 at duty, 4 rifle grenade, 2 bombed, 1 aerial torpedo, 1 bullet). The brigade commander is listed as a certain 'Captain, Brigade Major B. L. Montgomery (later Alamein)'.

Montgomery of Alamein! We used to watch him on the television – 'ghastly little Monty poncing about in black and white', as my brother put it – explaining how he had won the Second World War. My brother and I used to mimic his inability to pronounce his *r*s. 'I then gave Wommel a wight hook', would be our mock summary of the Desert Campaign. Grandpa never told us he had served under Monty – never even told his own daughter, who would certainly have mentioned it as part of family history every time we tuned in.

The brigade's diary for 17 November 1916 notes: 'The Army Commander has lately seen a very short-sighted man in a Battalion of Infantry and a deaf man in another. These would be a danger in the front line.' (There's a novel would-you-rather: would you rather be deaf or blind in the First World War?) Another note from Command states: 'The number of courts martial held in the Division during the period 1st Dec. 1916 to date tend to show that the state of discipline in the Division is not what it should be.' Over that period the 17th Lancashire Fusiliers had 1 desertion, 6 Sleeping on Post and 2 'accidental' (presumably self-inflicted) injuries.

There is no evidence – there could be no evidence – that my grandfather featured in these statistics. He was an ordinary soldier who volunteered, was shipped out to France for the middle period of the war, and progressed from private to sergeant. He was invalided out with (as I have always understood it) trench foot or feet, 'a painful condition caused by prolonged immersion in water or mud, marked by swelling, blistering, and some degree of necrosis'. He returned to England at an unspecified date, and was discharged on 13 November 1917, along with twenty others from his regiment, as 'No longer physically fit for service.' He was then twenty-eight, and oddly – I assume mistakenly – listed as a private in the records of discharge. And despite my brother's memory, he did receive medals, if of the lowliest kind – the kind awarded for simply turning up: the British War Medal, given for entering a theatre of war, and the Victory Medal, given to all eligible personnel who served in an operational theatre. The latter reads, on its reverse, 'The Great War for Civilization 1914–1919.'

And there it all runs out, memory and knowledge. These are the available scraps; nothing more can be known. But since family piety is not my motivation, I am not disappointed. I give my grandfather's service, and its secrets, and his silence, as an example. First, of being wrong: thus I discovered that 'Bert Scoltock, so christened, so called, so cremated', in fact began life, in April 1889, at the register office of Driffield in the County of York, as Bertie; and was still Bertie in the census of 1901. Secondly, as an example of how much you can find out, and where that leaves you. Because what you can't find out, and where that leaves you, is one of the places where the novelist starts. We (by which I mean 'I') need a little, not a lot; a lot is too much. We begin with a silence, a mystery, an absence, a contradiction. If I had discovered that Grandpa had been one of the six Sleeping on Post, and that while he was slumbering the enemy had crept up and slaughtered some of his fellow Fusiliers, and that this had caused him great Remorse, a feeling he had carried to the grave (and if I were to discover all this from a hand-written affidavit – mark that remorsefully shaky signature – while clearing out an old bank-deposit box), I might have been satisfied as a grandson, but not as a novelist. The story, or the potential story, would have been spoilt. I know a writer who likes to linger on park benches, listening in to conversations; but as soon as his eavesdropping threatens to disclose more than he professionally requires, he moves on. No, the absence, the mystery, they are for us (him and me) to solve.

So in 'Scenes from Highways & Byways', my eye is drawn not to Great Uncle Percy in Blackpool or Nurse Glynn or Sgt P. Hyde Killed in Action Dec 1915 but to the lips and hair and white blouse of 'Sept 1915' and the erasure beside the date. Why was this photograph defaced, and its edges ripped as if by raging fingernails? And further, why was it not either removed from the album entirely, or at least pasted over with another photograph? Here are some possible explanations: 1. It was a picture of Grandma, which Grandpa liked, but which she later took against. However, this wouldn't explain the seeming violence of the attack, which has dug through to the album page below. Unless, 1b., it was done after senility took hold, and Grandma had simply failed to recognize herself. Who is this woman, this interloper, this temptress? And so she scratched herself out. But if so, why this picture rather than any other? And why erase the scrap of information next to the date? 2. If this was another woman, was the gouging done by Grandma? If so, roughly when? Shortly after she was stuck into the album, as a dramatic marital strike? Much later, but in Grandpa's lifetime? Or after Grandpa's death, as a long-delayed act of revenge? 3. Could this, just possibly, be 'a very nice girl called Mabel', after whom my mother was named? What did Grandma once tell my mother – that there would be no bad men in the world if there were no bad women. 4. Grandpa might have done the gouging and attempted ripping himself. This seems highly unlikely as a) it was his album; b) he was experienced in handicrafts, leatherwork and bookbinding, and would certainly have made a better job of it; and c) photo-mutilation is, I suspect, a predominantly female crime. 5. But in any case, consider the dates. Bert (as he had become by 1914) and Nell were married the day war broke out; their daughter was conceived within a month, and born in June 1915. The mystery photograph is dated September 1915. My grandfather volunteered in November 1915, though conscription was to be introduced anyway within a couple of months. Is this, perhaps, the reason he knew about remorse? And my mother, of course, was an only child.

A Bertie who changed into a Bert; a late volunteer; a mute witness; a sergeant discharged as a private; a defaced photograph; a possible case of remorse. This is where we work, in the interstices of ignorance, the land of contradiction and silence, planning to convince you with the seemingly known, to resolve – or make usefully vivid – the contradiction, and to make the silence eloquent.

MY GRANDFATHER PROPOSES, '"Friday. Worked in garden. Planted potatoes."' My grandmother retorts, 'Nonsense,'

and insists, '"Rained all day. Too wet to work in garden."'
He shook his head when his *Daily Express* told him of a Red
Plot to Rule the World; she tut-tutted when her *Daily Worker*
warned her about US Imperialist Warmongers Sabotaging
People's Democracies. We all – their grandson (me), the
reader (you), even my last reader (yes, you, you bastard) –
are confident that the truth lies somewhere in between. But
the novelist (me again) is less interested in the exact nature
of that truth, more in the nature of the believers, the manner in which they hold their beliefs, and the texture of the
ground between the competing narratives.

Fiction is made by a process which combines total free-
dom and utter control, which balances precise observation
with the free play of the imagination, which uses lies to tell
the truth and truth to tell lies. It is both centripetal and cen-
trifugal. It wants to tell all stories, in all their contrariness,
contradiction and irresolvability; at the same time it wants
to tell the one true story, the one that smelts and refines and
resolves all the other stories. The novelist is both bloody
back-row cynic and lyric poet, drawing on Wittgenstein's
austere insistence – speak only of that which you can truly
know – and Stendhal's larky shamelessness.

An anecdote about my brother and me. When we were
little, he used to put me on my tricycle, blindfold me, and
push me as fast as possible into a wall. I was told this by my
niece C., who had it from her father. I have absolutely no
memory of it myself, and am not sure what, if anything, to
deduce from it. But let me dissuade you from an immediate

conclusion. It sounds to me like the sort of game I would have enjoyed. I can imagine my yelp of pleasure as the front tyre hit the wall. Perhaps I even suggested the game, or pleaded for it to be replayed. Without the kind of psychotherapeutic intervention of which I am suspicious, can I discover whether my non-memory comes from deliberate suppression (trauma! terror! fear of my brother! love of my brother! both!) or the unexceptionality of the event. My elder niece C. first described it to me, at the time she and I were dealing with my mother's final decline. She said that she and her sister were told it 'as a funny story' when they were little. But she did also remember concluding 'that it was not a particularly good way to behave, so perhaps he [her father, my brother] intended it as a cautionary tale of sorts'. If so, what might be the moral? Treat your younger sibling better than I did? Learn that life is like being pushed blindfold into a wall?

I apply to my brother for his version. 'The trike story,' he replies. 'I told it, or versions of it, to C. & C. to make them laugh – which, I fear, it did (I can't recall ever telling them anything with a moral to it . . .).' Now, there's having a philosopher for a father. 'In my memory, it was a game we played in the back garden at Acton. An obstacle course was set up on the lawn – logs, tincans, bricks. The game was to tricycle round the course without serious injury. One of us steered the trike while the other one pushed. (I think the trike had lost its chain; but perhaps the pushing aspect added to the sadistic pleasures of the event.) The steerer was blindfolded. I'm pretty sure we took it in turns to steer and to push; but I suspect that I pushed you faster than you pushed me. I don't recall any major accident (nor even anyone being pushed into a wall – which in fact would not have been at all easy, given the layout of the garden). I don't recall your being frightened. I seem to think we thought it was fun, and rather naughty.'

My niece's initial summary of the game – my brother blindfolding me before pushing me into a wall – might be a child's shorthand memory, emphasizing what she herself would most have feared; or it might be a subsequent abbreviation or reimagining made in the light of her relationship with her father. What's more surprising is that my own memory is blindfold, especially given the elaborateness of the proceedings. I wonder how my brother and I can have acquired logs and cans and bricks from our very small, neat suburban garden, let alone laid out such a course, without it being known and noted, and permitted or forbidden. But my niece rejects this: 'I'm sure your parents never told me the story; in fact, I thought they never knew about it.'

I apply to her younger sister. She too remembers the obstacle course, the blindfolding, the frequency of the game. 'You were then pushed at breakneck speed through the obstacles and the race ended with you being rammed into the garden wall. It was billed as a Great Bit of Fun for both of you, with an undercurrent of doing something that was certainly disapproved of by Mother; I think not so much because of the damage inflicted on you but the misuse of

garden tools and the soiling of washing hanging up to dry. I
don't know why we were told this story (or why I remember
it). I think it was the only story about you, in fact about the
family at all, except for your grandmother vomiting on a
boat into a series of yoghurt pots. I think it was supposed to
prove to us that children should do whatever they please, in
particular if it is silly and displeasing to adults . . . The story
was told in a jokey way and we were certainly supposed to
laugh and applaud the daring nature of the whole thing. I
don't think we ever questioned the truth of it all.'

You see (again) why (in part) I am a novelist? Three
conflicting accounts of the same event, one by a participant, two based on memories of subsequent retellings
thirty years ago (and containing detail the original teller
might himself have since forgotten); the sudden insertion
of new material – 'misuse of garden tools', 'soiling of washing'; the emphasis, in my nieces' versions, on a ritual
climax to the game – me being pushed into a wall – that my
brother denies; the forgetting of the whole episode by its
second participant, despite his serfdom as a log-trundler
and brick-gatherer; the absence, from my nieces' versions,
of a return match in which I got to push the trike; and most
of all, the moral variation between what my brother said
he had been intending when he told the story (pure amuse-
ment), and what his daughters, separately and differently,
concluded he was doing. My informants' replies might
almost have been scripted to cast doubt on the reliability
of oral history. And I am left with a new proposed

definition of what I do: a novelist is someone who remembers nothing yet records and manipulates different versions of what he doesn't remember.

The novelist in the present instance would need to supply the following: who invented the game; how the trike lost its chain; how the pusher instructed the unseeing driver to steer; whether or not Mother Really Knew; which garden tools were used; how the washing got soiled; what sadistic and/or pre-sexual pleasures might have been involved; and why it was the main, almost the only story a philosopher told about his childhood. Also, if the novel were to be multi-generational, whether the two sisters who first heard it subsequently repeated it to their own daughters (and with what humorous or moral purpose) – whether the story dies out, or is changed again in the mouths and minds of a subsequent generation.

For the young – and especially the young writer – memory and imagination are quite distinct, and of different categories. In a typical first novel, there will be moments of unmediated memory (typically, that unforgettable sexual embarrassment), moments where the imagination has worked to transfigure a memory (perhaps that chapter in which the protagonist learns some lesson about life, whereas in the original the novelist-to-be failed to learn anything), and moments when, to the writer's astonishment, the imagination catches a sudden upcurrent and the weightless, wonderful soaring that is the basis for fiction delightfully happens.

These different kinds of truthfulness will be fully apparent to the young writer, and their joining together a matter of anxiety. For the older writer, memory and the imagination begin to seem less and less distinguishable. This is not because the imagined world is really much closer to the writer's life than he or she cares to admit (a common error among those who anatomize fiction) but for exactly the opposite reason: that memory itself comes to seem much closer to an act of the imagination than ever before. My brother distrusts most memories. I do not mistrust them, rather I trust them as workings of the imagination, as containing imaginative as opposed to naturalistic truth. Ford Madox Ford could be a mighty liar, and a mighty truth-teller, at the same time, and in the same sentence.

CHITRY-LES-MINES LIES SOME twenty miles south of Vézelay. A faded blue tin sign proposes a right turn off the main road to *Maison de Jules Renard*, where the boy grew up amid a silent parental war and, years later, the man broke down the bedroom door to find his suicided father. A second tin sign, and a second right turn, leads you to *Monument de Jules Renard*, whose erection he teasingly entrusted to his sister a few months before he died: 'We were wondering this morning who would see to setting up my bust on the little square in Chitry. We thought straight away that we could count on you . . .' The 'little square', a lime-planted triangle in front of the church, has inevitably become the Place Jules Renard. The writer's bronze bust is supported by a stone column, at the base of which sits his fictional child alter-ego, a brooding Poil de Carotte, looking melancholy and mature for his age. A stone tree climbs up the other side of the column, bursting into leaf around the writer's shoulders: nature enclosing and protecting him, in death as in life. It is a handsome piece of work, and when unveiled in October 1913 by André Renard – pharmacist, former socialist deputy and distant cousin – it must have seemed the only monument this obscure village would ever require. Its size fits the square, and so renders the First World War memorial, only a few yards away, almost apologetic of its presence, its listed names somehow less important, and less of a loss to Chitry, than its arteriosclerotic chronicler.

There is not a shop, a café or even a grimy petrol pump in this straggly village; the only reason for an outsider to stop here is Jules Renard. Somewhere nearby must be the well, doubtless long since filled in, which claimed Mme Renard nearly a century ago. A tricolore on the building opposite the church identifies the *mairie* where both François Renard and his son performed their civic functions, where Jules was kissed on the lips by a bride he had just joined in matrimony ('It cost me 20 francs'). The tarmacked lane between *mairie* and *église* leads out of the village a few hundred yards to the cemetery, which still lies in open countryside.

It is a July day of canicular heat, and the square, sloping graveyard is as bleak and dusty as a parade round. A list of names and plot numbers is posted at the gate. Failing to realize that this refers to concessions about to expire, I look at first for the wrong Renard in the wrong plot. The cemetery's only other (living) occupant is a woman with a watering can, moving slowly among her favoured graves. I ask her where the writer might be found. 'He's down there on the left, next to the tap,' is her reply.

The village's most famous inhabitant is indeed tucked away in a corner of the graveyard. I remember that Renard *père* was the first person to be buried here without any religious ceremony. Perhaps that is why the family grave seems positioned a little below the salt, or next to the tap (if the tap was there then). It is a square plot, backed against the boundary wall, and protected by a low, green-painted iron railing; the little gate in the middle sticks from successive repaintings, and requires a certain force. Two stone planters sit just inside this gate. The squat tomb lies horizontally across the rear of the plot, and is surmounted by a large stonework book, open at a double page on which are inscribed the names of those lying beneath.

And here they all are, six of them anyway. The father who didn't speak to his wife for thirty of their forty married years, who laughed at the notion that he might kill himself with a pistol, and used a shotgun instead. The brother who imagined that his mortal enemy was the central heating system in his office, who lay on a couch with the Paris telephone directory propping his inert head, and whose end made Jules angry at 'death and its imbecile tricks'. The mother, silenced at last after a garrulous life by an 'impenetrable' death. The writer who used them all. The wife who as a widow burnt a third of her husband's *Journal*. The daughter who never married and was buried here in 1945 under her nickname Baïe. This was the last time they opened the deep pit at whose edge Jules had seen a fat worm strutting on the day his brother Maurice was interred.

In the last year of his life, when he knew himself condemned, Jules Renard took to visiting cemeteries. One day he went to see the Goncourt Brothers in their Montmartre tomb. The younger brother had been buried there in 1870; the elder, Edmond, in 1896, after a graveside eulogy from the death-fearing Zola. Renard noted in his *Journal* how the brothers' literary pride was such that they disdained mention of their profession. 'Two names, two sets of dates, they thought that was enough. *Hé! hé!*' Renard comments, in that curious French transcription of a cackle. 'That's not anything you can rely upon.' But did such plainness denote vanity – the assumption that everyone would know who they were – or its very opposite, a proper avoidance of boastfulness? Also, perhaps, a sober awareness that, once released into history, no writer's name is guaranteed?

Looking at the vault, thinking of all the Renards crammed in together – only the writer's sister Amélie and son Fantec escaped – and remembering their history of wrangling, hatred and silence, it strikes me that Goncourt would be justified in returning a *Hé! hé!* back at his younger colleague: for the company he is keeping, for that embarrassing sculptural cliché of the open stone book, for the naff planters. And then there is the inscription beneath which Renard lies. It begins, unsurprisingly, *'Homme de lettres'*, after which you might expect, in a filial echo, *'Maire de Chitry'*. Instead, the writer's subsidiary identification is as a member *'de l'Académie Goncourt'*. It feels like a tiny flicker of revenge for that diary entry: '. . . they thought that was enough'.

I look again at the stone planters. One is quite empty, the other contains a stunted yellow conifer, whose colour seems to mock any idea of keeping the memory green. This grave is no more visited than that of the Goncourts, though the proximity of the tap must bring a little passing traffic. I notice that there is still room on the stone book for a few more entries, so go back to the woman with the watering can and ask if there are any Renard descendants still in the village or its environs. She doesn't think so. I mention that no one has been added to the vault since 1945. 'Ah,' she replies, not entirely apropos, 'I was in Paris then.'

It doesn't matter what they put on your tomb. In the hierarchy of the dead it is visitor numbers that count. Is there anything sadder than an unvisited grave? On the second anniversary of his father's death, a mass was said for him in Chitry; only three old women from the village attended; Jules and his wife took a glazed earthenware wreath to the grave. In his *Journal*, he noted: 'We give the dead metal flowers, the flowers that last.' He went on: 'It is less cruel never to visit the dead than to stop going after a certain time.' Here we are less in the territory of 'What

In the hierarchy of the dead it is visitor numbers that count. Is there anything sadder than an unvisited grave?

they would have wanted' than of 'How would they have reacted had they known?' What will happen to my brother if he gets his wish of a garden grave when his widow is also dead and the house is sold? Who wants a decomposing Aristotle expert turning slowly into mulch?

There is something crueller than leaving the dead unvisited. You may lie in a *concession perpetuelle* for which you have paid, but if no one comes to see you, there is no one to hire a lawyer to defend you when the municipality decides that perpetual doesn't always or necessarily mean perpetual. Then, even here, you will be asked to make way for others, to renounce finally the occupation of space on this earth, to stop saying, 'I was here too.'

So here's another logical inevitability. Just as every writer will have a last reader, so every corpse will have a last visitor. By whom I don't mean the man driving the earth-digger who scoops out your remnants when the graveyard is sold off for suburban housing. I mean that distant descendant; or, in my own case, that gratifyingly nerdy (or rather, charmingly intelligent) graduate student – still bibliophilic long after reading has been replaced by smarter means of conveying narrative, thought, emotion – who has developed a quaint and lonely (or rather, entirely admirable) attachment to long-forgotten novelists of the distant Print Era. But a last visitor is quite different from a last reader. Grave visiting is not an emulative pastime; you do not swap suggestions like swapping stamps. So I shall thank my student in advance for having made the trip, and not ask what he or she really thinks of my books, or book, or anthologized paragraph, or of this sentence. Perhaps, like Renard when he went to Montmartre to see the Goncourts, my last visitor will have taken to cemetery-tramping after being given a death-warning, a Fayum moment, by the doctor; in which case, my sympathies.

Were I to receive such a diagnosis myself, I doubt I should start visiting the dead. I have done enough of that already, and shall have eternity (or at least, until perpetuity no longer means what it says) in their company. I'd rather spend time with the living; and with music, not books. And in those last days I must try to verify a number of things. Whether I smell of fish, for a start. Whether dread takes over. Whether consciousness splits – and whether I shall be able to recognize it if it does. Whether I feel like forgiveness, memory-invoking, funeral planning. Whether remorse descends, and if it can be dispelled. Whether I am tempted – or deceived – by the idea that a human life is after all a narrative, and contains the proper satisfactions of a decent novel. Whether courage means not scaring others, or something considerably greater and probably out of reach. Whether I have got this death thing straight – or even a little straighter. And whether, in the light of late-arriving information, this book needs an afterword – one in which the *after* is stressed more heavily than usual.

So that's the view from here, now, from what, if I am lucky, if my parents are any sort of guide, might be three-quarters of the way through my life; though we know death to be contradictory, and should expect any railway station, pavement, overheated office or pedestrian crossing to be called Samarra. Premature, I hope, to write: farewell me. Premature also to scribble that graffito from the cell wall: I was here too. But not premature to write the words which, I realize, I have never put in a book before. Not here, anyway, on the last page:

THE END

Or does that look a little loud? Perhaps better in upper and lower case:

The End

No, that doesn't look . . . final enough. A last would-you-rather, but an answerable one.

Note to printer: small caps, please.

THE END

Yes, I think that's more like it. Don't you?

JB
London, 2005–7

© Alan Edwards

JULIAN BARNES is one of Britain's most famous, best-loved writers. His first book was published when he was 34; before then, he was a lexicographer and a TV critic. His work is extremely diverse – he writes novels, stories and non-fiction – but it is the idea of mortality that has most continually preoccupied him.

Nothing To Be Frightened Of (from which this book is taken) puzzles over life's great unimaginable, inevitable conclusion and is also a memoir of Barnes's family. *Levels of Life* is his deeply moving portrait of losing a beloved wife. His most recent novel, *The Noise of Time* and his Booker Prize-wining, *The Sense of an Ending*, also deal with the theme of death.

Barnes has long been a fan of Leicester City Football Club. He lives in London.

RECOMMENDED BOOKS BY JULIAN BARNES:

Levels of Life
The Sense of an Ending
The Noise of Time

How do we cope with Death?

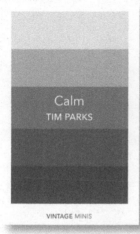

Calm
TIM PARKS

VINTAGE MINIS

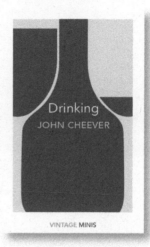

Drinking
JOHN CHEEVER

VINTAGE MINIS

Babies
ANNE ENRIGHT

VINTAGE MINIS

Psychedelics
ALDOUS HUXLEY

VINTAGE MINIS

VINTAGE MINIS

The Vintage Minis bring you the world's greatest writers on the experiences that make us human. These stylish, entertaining little books explore the whole spectrum of life – from birth to death, and everything in between. Which means there's something here for everyone, whatever your story.

vintageminis.co.uk